Dr. Cliff Boone

Foreword by Daniel Henderson

CHRIST
VICTORIOUS

How to Experience Christ's Victory over the Devil in Your Everyday Life

WESTBOW
PRESS®
A DIVISION OF THOMAS NELSON
& ZONDERVAN

Interior Image Credit: Ron DiCianni

WestBow Press books may be ordered through booksellers or by contacting:

WestBow Press
A Division of Thomas Nelson & Zondervan
1663 Liberty Drive
Bloomington, IN 47403
www.westbowpress.com
1 (866) 928-1240

ISBN: 978-1-9736-3652-6 (sc)
ISBN: 978-1-9736-3651-9 (hc)
ISBN: 978-1-9736-3653-3 (e)

Library of Congress Control Number: 2018909658

Print information available on the last page.

WestBow Press rev. date: 09/25/2018

CONTENTS

Dedicated to:

Steven Bennett Boone
Twice My Brother

ACKNOWLEDGEMENTS

Sprinkled throughout this book are stories told by people about their experiences with the unseen realm. All the stories are true; however, for privacy's sake, I have changed the names. Most of the stories were written by the people themselves. In some of the cases, I wrote the story down after hearing it firsthand. In all the cases, I've edited the words slightly to make them more appropriate for publication. I have not included any third-hand stories. These all occurred either in my own life or in the life of someone I know personally. I thank you who have told your stories—for your honesty and willingness to share.

In terms of logistics, this book would not be in your hands except for the special contribution of a few dedicated people. Barbara Carney repeatedly, and with great generosity of spirit, edited the mechanics of my writing. Ron Kohl provided helpful editorial suggestions and encouragement. Julie Sebastian contributed invaluable administrative help. Venus Gamboa, of WestBow Press, patiently shepherded me through the publishing process. My heartfelt thanks to you all.

I am grateful to those men who served as elders of Cedar Crest Bible Fellowship Church during part or all of the time I was working on this project—John Colabroy, Ron Erb, Pete Everett, Glenn Felty, Jim Hertzog, Jon King, Steve Klase, Dave Kohler, John Mays, Tim Moyer, Nelson Randolph, John Schleicher, Tim Sebastian, Dave Tress, Bill Walters, Dan Waterman, and Rick Whitmire. If they had not allowed me extended time away from other pastoral duties this book would not have happened. Thank you, brothers.

I also thank the people of our church for their prayers and enthusiasm. The gratitude they have shown for how this teaching has been of benefit has sustained my motivation and reinforced my conviction that this book is indeed needed.

Lastly, I want to thank my wife. Without Becky's continual encouragement, I wouldn't have begun, much less completed, this project. Thank you

FOREWORD
by Daniel Henderson

Spiritual warfare has been a topic that has surged and faded repeatedly in Christian writings, whether it be novels or more academic attempts to unpack the subject. As a pastor for three decades, I've seen everything from "soup to nuts" in the variety of efforts to address this important issue.

In my view, Cliff Boone is an eminently credible voice in this arena, and I am honored to introduce you to his timely book. Cliff's teachings are not just abstract theory cooked up in a seminary library. Nor are they rooted in unusual experiences that must be explained by cherry-picking verses to validate the strange. Cliff's love for the scriptures and solid theological training are deeply rooted. Yet his experiences, both as a missionary in Africa and a respected pastor in the U.S., bring just the right mix to shape a credible voice.

Cliff writes with a clear, caring pastoral voice. He's been asked repeatedly to minister to missionaries struggling to understand spiritual warfare in a practical, biblical way. He has been faithful and skilled in shepherding church members with a helpful blend of teaching, prayer and care as they learn what it really means to "resist the devil." The book is not aimed at turning everyone into an exorcist! It is biblically-based help for normal Christians in their everyday life.

This is important because for many modern Christians spiritual warfare is a blind spot, or at best, a point of contention and confusion. This is true for many reasons. Among them is the reality that our increasingly secular culture tends to deny the unseen realm. Some conservative Christian circles avoid robust biblical consideration of the devil and his demons. Other extreme camps drift into excess, losing a sense of solid biblical moorings altogether. The overall fear of the topic motivates many to ignore this teaching altogether.

We need the teaching contained in this book! It is not new teaching. Christians in other ages knew it. Around the world, Christians today know and practice it. But Christians in American churches are being bullied by the devil without knowing how to resist. .

What I love most about this book is the emphasis on the power and authority of Christ in the life of the average Christian. Yes, the book carefully teaches, as necessary, about the person and work of Satan. Beginning with the book's title, however, we are drawn to focus, not on the devil, but on *Christ Victorious*. You will likely find yourself worshiping as you read. Cliff consistently exalts the worthiness and sufficiency of Christ before the reader's eyes.

As you read this book, you will not be left to cower in fear. Rather, you will be equipped to live a courageous and worshipful life, resting in Christ's victory and resisting the devil's lies.

The Apostle Paul declared, "But thanks be to God, who in Christ always leads us in triumphal procession, and through us spreads the fragrance of the knowledge of him everywhere." (2 Corinthians 2:14). Later in that same letter he wrote, "For though we walk in the flesh, we are not waging war according to the flesh. For the weapons of our warfare are not of the flesh but have divine power to destroy strongholds. We destroy arguments and every lofty opinion raised against the knowledge of God, and take every thought captive to obey Christ." (2 Corinthians 10:3–5)

This book will equip you for daily conquest and "weaponize" you for a winning warfare as you stand firm in the full provision of Jesus Christ. I urge you to begin with expectation, read with care, and finish with confidence in the provision of Jesus for the gospel race set before you.

Daniel Henderson
President—www.strategicrenewal.com
Author—Transforming Prayer

1

GENESIS & MATTHEW

For still our ancient foe doth seek to work us woe.
His craft and power are great, and armed with
cruel hate, on earth is not his equal.

Martin Luther

We do not read very far into either the Old or the New Testaments before we are introduced to Satan.

In the first two chapters of Genesis, God speaks, and out of formlessness and darkness we see the heavens and earth come into being. Spinning through space the earth is a marvel of living diversity. In this paradise God specially creates the first man and woman, commissioning them to care for the rest of the earth.

Then quickly, in chapter 3, the tone changes when another being shows up to mar the wonder. Satan tempts our first parents. His attempt to do so is a success, and all the rebellion, sin and suffering that you and I experience is due to Satan's interference that day.

God created the world, put humans in a unique position, and Satan targeted the first man.

The first three chapters of Matthew are as full of wonder as the beginning of Genesis. A virgin gives birth. The child is the long-foretold Son of David and is affirmed by wise men who had been directed to him by signs in the heavens. Later he was baptized by a man whom an ancient prophet predicted.

Then quickly, in chapter 4, a being shows up to mar the wonder. His intent was already seen in chapter 3 when Herod attempted to kill the child. But here in chapter 4, rather than using others as his puppets, the being himself is present. In the wilderness Satan would attempt to do to the second man what he did to the first.[1]

God sent his Son into this world, put him in a unique position, and Satan targeted the second man.

But this time the devil failed. The second man—Jesus Christ—resists the devil and proceeds from the wilderness to the cross, from the cross to the resurrection, from the resurrection to the right of hand of the Father, and eventually will return to earth for the consummation of the devil's defeat.

The devil is brought to our attention early in both Testaments and is presented as part of the reality of our earthly life.

I find it intriguing that many Christians live with serious doubts as to the reality of Satan and the power of his influence on their lives. Some do not recognize anything in their weekly routine that they could attribute to the devil. Although they acknowledge that the Bible says that there is a devil, they function as if he is not real.

Others cloak their doubts with mistaken theology, justifying their lack of deliberate action against Satan with erroneous thoughts about a supposed Christian "spiritual immunity." In both cases, what results is a person who does not look like the Bible's portrait of a Christian. Scripture portrays us as deliberately resisting the devil and as wrestling with unseen powers.[2]

---

1   In 1 Corinthians 15:45 – 47 the Apostle Paul refers to Adam as the "first man" and to Jesus Christ as "the second man" or "the last Adam."

2   James 4:7; 1 Peter 5:9; Ephesians 6:10 – 18.

After over three decades of pastoral and missionary experience, I am no longer surprised to hear certain questions and concerns:

How can I tell if my temptation has a demonic element or is only because of my sinful self?

I know that we are told to resist the devil, but <u>how</u> do I do that?

How much influence can Satan have over a Christian?

Is there a way I can protect myself and my children?

Are my weird and frightening dreams because of evil spirits?

How do I recognize when I'm being attacked by the evil one?

This topic makes me afraid. Why can't I just ignore it?

There are answers.

God has taken my wife and me through various experiences that made us aware of the conflict with the demonic and that have driven us to the Bible for answers. Because we spent eleven years ministering in East Africa, people often assume that our experience with the unseen realm was learned there. It is true that our African brothers and sisters taught us much, and that the situations in which we found ourselves there seemed to have been orchestrated by God to instruct us in this area of the Christian life. But our "baptism" into this arena occurred in America before we left, and we have experienced the reality of the unseen realm continually in the years since we have returned. Demons need no passports. Satan is active in America just as much as anywhere else.

Over these decades I have wondered why certain attacks happened to me. Why did God allow me to encounter the demonic early in my Christian life and regularly during my ministry? I certainly was not seeking it. I did not want these experiences. Fear, of course, was a constant in these encounters. Confusion also played a big role. But due to wise counsel from older Christians, and an impetus to go to the Scriptures and find answers, I have come out of those encounters with an increasingly firm approach to resisting the devil. The fear is less; the victory is more. I am obeying the injunction to resist the devil, and I am seeing him flee.

Maybe the fact that you are holding this book in your hands is part of the answer as to why God put me into those trying situations. It is my prayer that what I have learned through these many years of wrestling may be used of God to help you too.

We ought not be discouraged or intimidated. The fact that Satan showed up early in both the Old and New Testaments does not mean that he prevails. There is a good end to the story! Eventually Satan is completely out of the picture.

Just two chapters away from the final verse of the Bible, we find Revelation 20:10, which says,

> And the devil who had deceived them was thrown
> into the lake of fire and sulfur where the beast and
> the false prophet were, and they will be tormented
> day and night forever and ever.

People argue over some of the details in that chapter, but the main point is clear and we must not miss it: the devil will be thrown into the lake of fire and will stay there forever!

One day the manifestation of Christ's victory over Satan will be complete and our wrestling will be over. In the meantime, we must learn to wrestle within the authority of the victorious Christ. Please allow me to show you how to do that.

2

A "PLACE"

*Till we sin Satan is a mere parasite; but when
once we are in the devil's hands he turns tyrant.*
Thomas Manton

If you knew that Satan was going to personally approach you within the next few hours, how would you feel? What would you tell your friends?

We see in John 14:30 that Jesus was in that exact situation. The Last Supper had concluded. In a matter of minutes, he and the disciples would head to Gethsemane. What he told the disciples at that moment is very instructive to anyone wishing to be equipped for the wrestling that we have with the devil. Jesus said, "I will not speak much more with you, for the ruler of the world is coming, and he has nothing in Me."[3]

"The ruler of the world is coming." Jesus knew that in just a short time, Satan himself would come to him. The discussions with his disciples would be put on hold. He would have to deal with Satan. What Jesus says next gives us important insight.

---

[3]   New American Standard Bible, Updated Edition.

Translators have struggled to put that last short phrase of John 14:30 into English. The English Standard Version puts it, "He has no claim on me." The New International Version reads, "He has no hold on me." Several versions translate it as, "He has no power over me." All of these wordings express truth, but they go beyond what the Greek text of Scripture actually says. In this case the simple words, taken as they are, give us more help than the translators' attempts to explain them.

A straightforward translation of this phrase into English is: "And in me he has nothing." Satan was coming to tempt Jesus in order to derail all the purposes that God had in sending Christ to earth. Jesus knew this, but simply said, "In me he has nothing." Satan had nothing—no thing—in Christ.

Please pause and carefully consider this. Jesus is implying that the strategy of Satan is to find something in the person whom he is attacking. This "something" can be likened to a foothold that gives the devil leverage in the person's life. He is looking for some sort of opportunity within the person he is targeting. Our Lord, being the sinless Son of God and wholly obedient Son of Man, had no such foothold within him. He would face Satan's fury and scheming and terror with absolutely no advantage given over to the enemy.

One of my daughters and her husband are rock climbers. I marvel at their ability to move across high rock faces, securing themselves by gripping tiny ledges. When Satan approached Jesus, there was no ledge for Satan to grip—not even a fingernail's width of a ledge. "In me he has nothing."

But the same cannot be said of you and me. The Apostle Paul was aware of our danger, and under the inspiration of the Holy Spirit, he wrote about it. Consider his words in Ephesians 4:26 – 27. "Be angry and do not sin; do not let the sun go down on your anger, and give no opportunity to the devil."

Here again, understanding the Greek language is helpful. The word that is translated in this verse as "opportunity" is the Greek word for "place." Some English versions of the Bible actually use the word "place" here, while still others translate the word as "foothold." The point is that it is correct to translate verse 27 as "and give no place to the devil."

I am convinced that the reference to a "place" here in Ephesians 4:27 is the same thing that Jesus was talking about in John 14:30. Satan had no "place" in Jesus where he could gain an advantage or find an opportunity. There was no foothold in our Savior. But we give our enemy footholds all the time.

Note the circumstances in which Paul warns us of giving a place to Satan.

> You...were taught in him...to put off your old self, which belongs to your former manner of life and is corrupt through deceitful desires...and to put on the new self, created after the likeness of God in true righteousness and holiness.

> Therefore, having put away falsehood, let each one of you speak the truth with his neighbor, for we are members one of another. Be angry and do not sin; do not let the sun go down on your anger, and give no opportunity to the devil. Let the thief no longer steal, but rather let him labor, doing honest work with his own hands, so that he may have something to share with anyone in need. Let no corrupting talk come out of your mouths, but only such as is good for building up, as fits the occasion, that it may give grace to those who hear. And do not grieve the Holy Spirit of God, by whom you were sealed for the day of redemption. Let all bitterness and wrath and anger and clamor and slander be put away from you, along with all malice. Be kind to one another,

tenderhearted, forgiving one another, as God in
Christ forgave you.[4]

The Apostle is giving us a list of what to put out of our lives:
falsehood, unchecked anger, stealing, unwholesome talk, bitterness, etc.
When he mentions anger, he adds this insight: unchecked anger gives
the devil a *place* in our lives. He is warning us that as we are learning
to put off the sinful practices of our pre-Christian life, the devil waits
nearby ready to take advantage of any opportunity we give him.

Anger, for the right reasons and aimed at the right occasion, is
not necessarily sinful. Unchecked anger, however, is dangerous. If we
don't control it, it easily begins to control us. Worse than that, the
devil then sees an opportunity and establishes a foothold in that life.

Although Paul has explicitly linked the sin of unchecked anger
to the giving of an opportunity to the devil, I believe that other sins
can also be doorways through which the evil one attains influence
in our lives. As a matter of fact, it is my observation that any sin
that has become habitual is highly likely to have provided the evil
one an avenue into one's life. The very fact that the sin has become a
habit means that the person has abdicated his or her will in the case
of that particular temptation. Satan exploits passive wills. Anger in
particular, and all habitual sins, give a place to the devil.

But to whom is Paul talking? He is consistent throughout the
book of Ephesians. When he says "you" or "us" he is referring to men
and women who have heard the gospel, believed in Jesus Christ, and
been sealed with the Holy Spirit.[5] He is referring to those whom God
has made alive together with Christ.[6] He is speaking to Christians—
genuine, real Christians.

---

[4]   Ephesians 4:21 – 32.

[5]   Ephesians 1:13 "In him you also, when you heard the word of truth,
       the gospel of your salvation, and believed in him, were sealed with the
       promised Holy Spirit."

[6]   Ephesians 2:4 – 5 "But God, being rich in mercy, because of the great
       love with which he loved us, even when we were dead in our trespasses,

Genuine Christians can give a place to the devil in their own lives. This uncomfortable truth is what the Bible teaches. This does not mean, however, that defeat is certain. God directed the Apostle Paul and other biblical writers to instruct us concerning how to come out on the winning side in this life-long conflict with evil. There is an evil being who seeks our destruction, but there is a way to take back any place we've given him, to keep that from happening again, and to live in the power of spiritual freedom.

Craig's Story

What I want to share with you is embarrassing, but true. I've been a Christian for many years. I'm married to a great wife and we're raising our children as best as we know how. My work is mentally tiring, and when I get home in the evening, I just want to turn my mind off. There was a period of time when I started playing an online puzzle game. It was mindless and harmless, or so I thought. At times my conscience told me that I was spending too much time playing that stupid game. I'd come home from work, tell my family hello, say I wanted to rest, and then go to my room and start playing the game. Sometimes someone from the family would knock on my door, and I'd quick change the screen before they saw what I was doing. When I look back on it now, it seems so ridiculous, but that is what was happening. I played it so much that when I'd

made us alive together with Christ—by grace you have been saved."

close my eyes at night to go to sleep, images from the game would buzz across my eyes. It was like I had burned them into my eyeballs! Eventually, I experienced headaches and eye pain. I told myself that I would change, and tried, but it seemed like the pull to play the game always won. Daily I wound up playing that game again. Finally, I came to grips with the situation and realized that I was wasting time, losing opportunity to be with my family, harming my body, and going against my own conscience. And I wasn't in charge of myself anymore. I remembered 1 Corinthians 6:12, which says, "'All things are lawful for me,' but not all things are helpful. 'All things are lawful for me,' but I will not be enslaved by anything." I was enslaved by this silly online computer game, and I wanted to be free. So I got on my knees and asked God's forgiveness, determined not to do the game anymore, and resisted the devil like our pastor had taught us. The pull to play that game was lessened, and I've never clicked on that website again. Praise the Lord!

3

THE DEVIL'S INTENT

Let us watch Satan for he watches us. We are naturally afraid of a physical enemy, but our spiritual foe appears less terrible because we are less aware of him.

Thomas Adams

For most of my high school and college years I was a wrestler. It was exhilarating to pit my skill and strength against someone else's in the one-on-one intensity of a wrestling match! Wrestling is a rough sport. My mom never really enjoyed watching for fear that I would get injured, and sometimes when I would grapple with an opponent, one of us would get hurt. I can honestly say, however, that I never intentionally hurt an opponent. I'm not sure the same thing can be said for all those who wrestled against me, but I can say this: no one was trying to kill me. It was a sport, and as intense and painful as it could become, it always remained a sport. We weren't gladiators battling to the death; we were wrestlers trying to outscore one another.

Not so with the devil. He is not trying to outscore us. His intent is to destroy us.

Twice Jesus taught us about the intentions of the devil. In John 8:44, while addressing those who were opposing him, he said, "You are of your father the devil, and your will is to do your father's desires. *He was a murderer from the beginning.*"

He is a murderer. He aims for our death. He wants to kill all those who have been created in the image of God. When someone believes in Jesus Christ, the devil has failed in his attempt to lead that person into eternal death. But the devil's intent is still the same, and he will attempt to kill all the good that God would do in and through that believer.

In John 10:10 Jesus said, "The thief comes only *to steal and kill and destroy.* I came that they may have life and have it abundantly."

The intent of the devil is to steal—to take what rightfully belongs to another.

The intent of the devil is to kill—to extinguish life.

The intent of the devil is to destroy—to ruin and render useless.

He often pursues this goal of destruction methodically and over a long period of time.

Ephesians 6:11 refers to "the schemes of the devil." A scheme is a detailed plan. Another term that could be used is "stratagem." You may not have thought about it this way before, but Satan plans against you. He puts forethought into a strategy on how he will destroy you.

In 2 Corinthians 2 Paul was counseling the church on how to receive back into their fellowship a person who had grievously sinned. In verse 11 he ended his advice with a reminder of why they should each do the right thing— "so that we would not be outwitted by Satan; for we are not ignorant of his designs." What an interesting and alarming use of words! Satan has "designs" against the people of God. He is plotting against us.

What I want you to understand from these verses is that Satan's activity in this world is more than a general, overarching, non-personal influence of evil. On the contrary, it is directed towards individuals and churches, and it is carried out with forethought and design by evil beings.

But we are not ignorant of these plots and strategies. Through Scripture and experience, we discern the devil's tactics, and thereby become less susceptible to them. One crucial element we must understand is that even in the temptations that we perceive as small, Satan's intent is destruction. He is willing to go small and get little victories in order to establish a place in your life. Once he has that place, he then attempts to leverage it, all with the goal of eventually throwing your entire life into disarray and destruction. He will start small. He will work slowly. But during the entire time he has one intent—your destruction.

Realizing this stratagem of our enemy changes the way we look at our own temptations. What seems like an insignificant compromise, like Craig's online game playing, is now seen as the dangerous first phase of an attack. It has the potential of resulting in the giving over of a place in the person's life that Satan will attempt to use towards his goal. He will seek to build a pattern of compromise until there is slavery in that one area of the life. Then he will use that foothold to broaden his influence, to move into other areas of that person's life. Mixed into this progression is deception. Deception and slavery work hand in hand, increasing sinful attitudes and actions. Eventually all sorts of consequences are experienced: relationships are broken, finances are ruined, health is lost, joy is gone, influence on others for good is absent—the one whose aim is to steal, kill and destroy has done just that. Yet we do not usually think of this big picture of the devil's strategy when we are presented with some small temptation.

This is disconcerting—to know that the devil is scheming against us with such murderous intent. What do we do? How can we be safe?

In the very passage in which Jesus spoke of the devil's intent, he was giving us confidence. I doubt those listening that day were left fearing, and we need not fear, either. Read these verses carefully. Jesus said,

> The thief comes only to steal and kill and destroy. I came that they may have life and have it abundantly. I am the good shepherd. The good shepherd lays down his life for the sheep. He who is a hired hand and not a shepherd, who does not own the sheep, sees the wolf coming and leaves the sheep and flees, and the wolf snatches them and scatters them. He flees because he is a hired hand and cares nothing for the sheep. I am the good shepherd. I know my own and my own know me, just as the Father knows me and I know the Father; and I lay down my life for the sheep.[7]

We have a shepherd who knows all about our enemy: all about his evil intent, and all about his stratagems. This shepherd loves us, calls us his own, and is so committed to us that he will lay down his life in order that our adversary does not destroy us. We do not fear being destroyed by Satan because we have Jesus and he has us.

In this book we must, out of necessity, place some of our attention on Satan, but my overarching intent is to leave you thinking about Jesus. Jesus is the one who successfully resisted the devil in the wilderness and in every temptation that followed. He died, sinless, on the cross. Satan never won when he attacked our Savior. Jesus is the only one who gave no place to Satan. The devil never had a millimeter's worth of leverage in Christ. The stratagems that the devil uses against us utterly failed when he tried to practice them against our Lord.

It is Jesus who faced off against Satan and won. No one else is our source of safety and victory. It would be a mistake to approach the

---

[7]   John 10:10 – 15.

whole subject of our wrestling with the devil under the assumption that our freedom is merely a matter of learning techniques: how to pray, how to resist, etc. Surely there is value in knowing those things, and I will teach you what I've learned about them, but more fundamental to our victory is Jesus himself.

Remember the story of those who tried to use Jesus' name to cast out demons but ended up bitterly regretting that they did?

> Then some of the itinerant Jewish exorcists undertook to invoke the name of the Lord Jesus over those who had evil spirits, saying, "I adjure you by the Jesus whom Paul proclaims." Seven sons of a Jewish high priest named Sceva were doing this. But the evil spirit answered them, "Jesus I know, and Paul I recognize, but who are you?" And the man in whom was the evil spirit leaped on them, mastered all of them and overpowered them, so that they fled out of that house naked and wounded.[8]

Not a pretty picture. It shows us that our conflict with evil is more than a matter of technique. They were using the name of Jesus, but they themselves were not in Jesus. How ironic, that while speaking the name of the Lord, they were not able to experience the truth that "the name of the Lord is a strong tower; the righteous man runs into it and is safe."[9]

Taking shelter in the name of the Lord means more than merely pronouncing his name. If we are truly in that shelter, however, we are safe.

---

[8]   Acts 19:13 – 16.
[9]   Proverbs 18:10.

4

IN CHRIST

Blessed be the God and Father of our Lord Jesus Christ, who has blessed us in Christ with every spiritual blessing.

Paul the Apostle

For many years I was aware of the sixth chapter of Ephesians and its well-known exhortation to stand firm amid our very real battle with evil beings. You are probably aware of it also. Let's remind ourselves of the first few verses of that famous passage:

> Finally, be strong in the Lord and in the strength of his might. Put on the whole armor of God, that you may be able to stand against the schemes of the devil. For we do not wrestle against flesh and blood, but against the rulers, against the authorities, against the cosmic powers over this present darkness, against the spiritual forces of evil in the heavenly places.[10]

---

[10]   Ephesians 6:10 – 11.

In these verses we immediately notice that a Christian's life is expected to involve conflict with the devil and his agents. The idea of spiritual conflict is not introduced by the Apostle Paul any differently than he introduced his other subjects. He had previously given instruction to Christians on how to live rightly as husbands and wives (5:22 – 33), parents and children (6:1 – 4), and slaves and masters (6:5 – 9), and now he takes up the issue of how to deal with the reality and power of the unseen realm. It is matter-of-fact for Paul. It is an expected part of the Christian life. It is not awe-inspiring, or curious, or weird…it is a normal part of life.

For many years I attempted to apply this passage of Scripture to my life without thinking about its connection to the rest of the book of Ephesians. I had never seen how what was said in earlier chapters helped me to put chapter six into action. This connection, once understood, lays the groundwork for experiencing the power of a crucial principle concerning our wrestling with Satan. Allow me to show you the connection and the principle.

In 1:15 – 21 we find one of those super-long sentences for which the Apostle Paul is famous. I'll quote a portion of it here beginning in verse 19:

> And what is the immeasurable greatness of his power toward us who believe, according to the working of his great might that he worked in Christ when he raised him from the dead and seated him at his right hand in the heavenly places, far above all rule and authority and power and dominion, and above every name that is named, not only in this age but also in the one to come.[11]

Notice that Christ has been exalted to God's right hand, which is described as being in the heavenly places. Notice too that being there, he is far above all the other spiritual beings.

---

[11]   Ephesians 1:19 – 21.

Then in 2:4 – 10 we see what has happened to us when we are saved:

> But God, being rich in mercy, because of the great love with which he loved us, even when we were dead in our trespasses, made us alive together with Christ—by grace you have been saved—and raised us up with him and seated us with him in the heavenly places in Christ Jesus.[12]

Notice what God has done with us. He "made us alive," "raised us up," and "seated us." Very important to understand, however, is that he did all of this to us "with Christ," or, as he states at the end of verse 6, "in Christ." He spiritually joined us to Christ and thus counts us as being in Christ's resurrection, ascension, and session.[13] We are where Christ is.

Right about now you may be struggling to follow what I am saying. This is very normal, partly because the concept is foreign to our daily experience, partly because the personal blessing of understanding it seems to correspond to our effort in pursuing it, and partly because there is resistance to it in the spiritual realm. Pray that God will help you see this truth, and don't stop trying to grasp it until God gives it to you.

Some are confused by the geographical nature of this sort of language. They say, "You are telling me that I am *in the heavenly places*, but I'm not in the heavenly places; I'm sitting right here!" We must realize that this language is not referring to our bodies but to our status before God. God officially recognizes us as being in Christ.

Being "in the Lord," we then engage in the struggle explained in 6:12: "For we do not wrestle against flesh and blood, but against the

---

12   Ephesians 2:4 – 6.
13   The "session of Christ" is a phrase referring to Christ having been seated at the right hand of the Father.

rulers, against the authorities, against the cosmic powers over this present darkness, against the spiritual forces of evil in the heavenly places." We wrestle the spiritual enemies from a position of advantage because we are in Christ.

I'll state it again. Christ is exalted far above all the evil powers. We are in Christ, so in terms of spiritual authority, we are positioned far above our enemies. We enter the conflict, therefore, from the position of advantage over them.

I have a favorite briefcase I've owned for years. If I put my phone in the briefcase, raise the briefcase up over my head, and then ask, "Where is my phone?" there could be two answers. Someone could either say, "Over your head" or "In the briefcase." Both answers are correct.

Let me ask you a question. From what vantage point do you resist the devil? There are two answers. One is "far above all rule and authority and power and dominion." The other answer is "in Christ." Both answers are correct.

Think with me again about the second answer: "In Christ." That is where we are, and it is from that vantage point that we successfully resist the devil. This is the principle from which we derive our strength for the battle.

Why then are we often defeated? There is an important, yet easily overlooked, reality in verse 10. We are straightforwardly commanded to "be strong in the Lord and in the strength of his might." Why would we be exhorted to do that unless there is a real possibility of entering the spiritual battle apart from the strength of the Lord? The deliberate reckoning of ourselves to be in Christ, and then the facing of our enemies in the strength that results from that reckoning, is what enables us to fight from a position of advantage over the evil one.

Some confusion about our warfare with Satan occurs because there is a lack of clarity concerning the distinction between what is done for us in the Christian life and what requires our participation. This lack of clarity can be especially evident when we consider a verse like Ephesians 6:10, which contains both a command and the phrase "in the Lord." I have heard it said that because it was God who put us in the Lord, it will be God who unilaterally gives us the necessary strength. But why then the command?

We know that it is the work of God that placed us in Christ.[14] We did not do that. It would be a mistake, therefore, to suggest that we are doing something to put ourselves in Christ in order to fight the spiritual fight. But that is not what Ephesians 6:10 is telling us to do. It is telling us to be active in gaining strength from our already-received position of being in Christ.

I am convinced that the exhortation of 6:10 is for us to reckon, or to re-affirm in our own mind, the truth of our position in Christ, and thus gain the necessary strength to stand firm against the enemy. We must actively claim our place in Christ when involved in demonic attacks. This reaffirmation, sometimes stated out loud in the presence of the evil one, aligns our thinking with truth, bolsters our faith, and brings down the enemy.

In Christ. That is where you will experience the victory.

---

[14] Ephesians 2:4 – 6 makes it clear that it was God, not us, who "made us alive together with Christ."

5

AUTHORITY VS. POWER

Certain it is, and we are to believe it by faith, that the power of Satan is not equal to the power of God. It is not so strong, so large, and so wide. It is every way infinitely less. There is no comparison between that which is infinite and that which is finite.

Arthur Dent

The tenth chapter of Luke begins with Jesus sending some of his followers out on a temporary preaching assignment. When they came back to report to Jesus, we find crucial instruction concerning our conflict with the evil one.

> The seventy-two returned with joy, saying, "Lord, even the demons are subject to us in your name!" And he said to them, "I saw Satan fall like lightning from heaven. Behold, I have given you authority to tread on serpents and scorpions, and over all the power of the enemy, and nothing shall hurt you.

Nevertheless, do not rejoice in this, that the spirits
are subject to you, but rejoice that your names are
written in heaven."[15]

Read these verses again with the following two questions in
mind: What is it that the enemy has? What is it that the followers
of Jesus were given?

Did you notice the difference in your answers? The enemy has
power ("And over all the power of the enemy."). The followers of
Jesus have *authority* ("Behold, I have given you authority."). The
distinction between these two is significant, and the help we gain
by understanding the distinction is immeasurable. We approach the
enemy in our authority, not in our power. We do not out-muscle
Satan. He is enormously stronger than we are. We defeat him by
standing in the proper authority.

On one occasion while driving my car, I approached an
intersection where the stoplights were not functioning. A policeman
was in the middle of the road directing traffic. As I neared the
junction, he faced me, held up his arm, put out his hand toward
my car with his palm facing me…and I stopped my car. Was it the
policeman's strength that stopped my car? Of course not. If I had
merely kept my foot on the gas pedal, I would have run him over! He
was not stronger than my automobile. I had more power than he did,
but he had authority over me. Behind him was all the power of the
State, and he was duly authorized by the State to tell me what to do
in that situation. In authority, he ordered me to stop, and I stopped.

So it is with you and the devil. He is stronger than you are, but
you have authority over him. You are in Christ. You are far above
the evil spiritual authorities, and above every name that is named.
When it is necessary, you can face the devil, and in the authority of
Jesus Christ, order him out. He will flee.

---

[15]   Luke 10:17 – 20.

Catherine's Story

We had prayed for our first child's birth and asked God to help her grow to love him. At one point when she was still a newborn, she began crying at night. Of course, it is normal for a baby to cry at night, but these cries seemed extra full of terror and she would not be soothed. My husband had to pick her up and get her to focus on his face, and finally she would calm down. It was very frightening. This was happening after a family member who had practiced voodoo had been visiting in our house. I called our pastor's wife to ask her how we should be praying. She told me I needed to claim the blood of Jesus and in His name, and out loud, command the evil spirits to get out! It worked!

I love how in the Word of God, we often find importance in the small words. It would seem to have been good enough to tell us that Christ was put in a place *above* other spiritual beings, but the Holy Spirit guided Paul to use a word that demands that we translate it, "*far* above."[16] That little word "far" makes a big difference. Christ is *far above* all other beings. No one else is close. When we stand in Christ and speak in his authority, the evil spirits must flee.

When in conflict with the devil or any of his agents, we are dealing in the realm of rights. When people are born again, they are no longer rightfully Satan's but have been taken out from under his

---

[16] Ephesians 1:21.

authority. God "has delivered us from the domain of darkness and transferred us to the kingdom of his beloved Son."[17] Why then does Satan still pursue footholds in our lives and try to exert influence on us?

Because he cheats.

He won't play by the rules unless he is caught. I enjoy watching two evenly talented football teams clash on the field. But it's not only the teams running up and down the gridiron—there are referees too. If the referees weren't there to throw the flag whenever a player breaks the rules, the whole game would degenerate into chaos. In the case of your spiritual life, you are the referee. Satan will cheat until you "throw the flag." When he sees that you recognize your authority and use it against him, he backs off. He has no right to be in your life, but he'll weasel himself into it if you let him. As my mentor and friend, Dr. Harold Burchett, often said, "Satan never passes by an open door."[18]

If you have put your faith in Jesus Christ, you are completely his, and Satan has no rightful claim on you. This truth is undoubtedly one reason why the New Testament speaks in such a fearlessly triumphant tone about the enemy and our conflict with him. It is true that we have a formidable foe, but it is equally true that we are safe and victorious in the Lord Jesus.

Your protection from Satan is not an accidental by-product of Jesus' work on earth. "The reason the Son of God appeared was to destroy the works of the devil."[19] Many Christians are used to thinking about the death of Christ in terms of what it did concerning sin, but not in terms of what it did to Satan. Jesus purposefully defeated Satan, and the ground of that victory is in the cross.

---

[17] Colossians 1:13.

[18] Harold Burchett has written two books that contain good insight concerning spiritual warfare: *People Helping People* and *Spiritual Life Studies*.

[19] 1 John 3:8.

It is important to realize the connection between Christ's death and Satan's defeat.

> God made [us] alive together with him, having forgiven us all our trespasses, by canceling the record of debt that stood against us with its legal demands. This he set aside, nailing it to the cross. He disarmed the rulers and authorities and put them to open shame, by triumphing over them in him.[20]

We owed a debt to the justice of God because of having broken his law. Under that condemnation we stood unprotected from the accusation and power of the evil one. When Christ substituted himself for us on the cross, our record of debt was canceled. "There is therefore now no condemnation for those who are in Christ Jesus."[21] Satan lost his advantage over us. He was disarmed because of Christ substituting himself for us on the cross.

When we find it necessary to resist the devil, we do so in the authority of Christ. We remind ourselves, and our enemy, that he has no right in our life and that he must flee when we resist. We wear the badge of heaven, hold up our hand, and say, "Stop!"

Brad's Story

One evening I was at home alone, didn't have anything important to do, and so turned on the television. There was a movie on that seemed vaguely interesting, so I put the remote

---

[20] Colossians 2:13 – 15.

[21] Romans 8:1.

aside and started watching. After only a few minutes, with no warning, a scene erupted on the screen that was an intense combination of sensuality and violence. I was so shocked that my head even went backwards like I had been struck. I fumbled with the remote until I finally shut off the TV. My heart rate was up. I felt out of breath. My spirit was reeling with what my eyes had seen. So, I began to pray. I asked God for forgiveness for any responsibility I bore and asked for his cleansing. There was a sense of oppression and weight that stayed with me. I kept asking God for his help, but the sense of darkness and uncleanness continued to weigh on me. I couldn't get the scenes out of my mind. Finally, I opened my mouth and said out loud, "Satan, in the authority of Jesus Christ, I resist you. I take back any ground that you gained in my life through this, and I order you out. Be gone! Because the Word of God says, 'Resist the devil and he will flee from you.'" The sense of oppression and uncleanness immediately left.

6

RESIST!

There can be no victory where there is no combat.
The victory lies not upon us but upon Christ, who
has taken it upon himself not only to conquer for
us, but also to conquer in us.

Richard Sibbes

The command in Scripture to resist the devil is just that—a command. Notice how the following two verses are worded.

"Submit yourselves therefore to God. *Resist the devil*, and he will flee from you."

"Be sober-minded; be watchful. Your adversary the devil prowls around like a roaring lion, seeking someone to devour. *Resist him*, firm in your faith."[22]

These are not suggestions, nor are they merely instructions. They are imperatives. God has ordered us to resist the devil.

As with any other command in Scripture, we are blessed if we obey, and we suffer negative consequences if we do not. Take, for example, the command "love one another." When we obey that

---

22   James 4:7; 1 Peter 5:8 – 9.

command, we and others benefit, but if we disobey, we all lose out. So it is with this command to resist the devil.

It is my observation that many American Christians are ill-equipped to obey this injunction, and we are suffering because of it. Unintentionally, we put this command in a different category than all of God's other commands. We readily accept our responsibility to obey what God tells us—except in this case. Because of our ignorance of the reality of demonic activity, the lack of teaching on this subject by our spiritual leaders, and our doubts about the unseen realm that are bolstered by generations of secular education, we read the command "resist the devil"—and then do nothing with it.

Let me say here that there is a preventative resisting of the devil that does not involve a direct confrontation with him. This kind of resistance involves the right use of the means of grace and the maintaining of a close personal walk with the Lord. I discuss this more fully in chapter 8, but for now I want to draw your attention to the fact that there are times in a Christian's life when a more direct, pointed resistance is needed.

Due to either a failure in our life, which has left a door open to the evil one, or an unprovoked spiritual attack in which the devil has targeted us, we can find ourselves in a situation in which we are facing the presence of evil. Something more than the daily and weekly habits of walking with Christ is needed. An evil spiritual being is actually present and exerting influence on us. The roaring lion is seeking to devour us, and we must actively resist him in order to prevail. How do we do that?

We begin to understand how to resist the devil by learning from the example of our Lord. Because of its importance, I will include the entire passage describing his encounter with Satan in the wilderness. Please read it carefully.

> Then Jesus was led up by the Spirit into the wilderness to be tempted by the devil. And after fasting forty days and forty nights, he was hungry.

And the tempter came and said to him, "If you are the Son of God, command these stones to become loaves of bread." But he answered, "It is written, 'Man shall not live by bread alone, but by every word that comes from the mouth of God.'" Then the devil took him to the holy city and set him on the pinnacle of the temple and said to him, "If you are the Son of God, throw yourself down, for it is written, 'He will command his angels concerning you,' and 'On their hands they will bear you up, lest you strike your foot against a stone.'" Jesus said to him, "Again it is written, 'You shall not put the Lord your God to the test.'" Again, the devil took him to a very high mountain and showed him all the kingdoms of the world and their glory. And he said to him, "All these I will give you, if you will fall down and worship me." Then Jesus said to him, "Be gone, Satan! For it is written, 'You shall worship the Lord your God and him only shall you serve.'" Then the devil left him, and behold, angels came and were ministering to him.[23]

There is great mystery in the incarnation of Christ. The eternal Son of God became a real human being. Although we cannot explicate in exact detail all the interplay of his divine and human natures, we can say this: he lived and ministered as the Perfect Man who was perfectly filled by the Holy Spirit. The general explanation for his life and ministry was not his deity but the perfection of his humanity in alignment with the Holy Spirit. Even his miracles are explained in this way by the Scripture.[24] I make this point to buttress

---

[23]   Matthew 4:1 – 11. It is also found in Luke 4:1 – 13.

[24]   Acts 2:22 and 10:38 attribute his miraculous works to the Spirit working through him as a man.

the assertion that his temptation in the wilderness does indeed serve as an example to you and me.

Also, we must not allow arguments about if he could actually have given into temptation to lure us away from the valuable lesson this Scripture has for us. Let us accept the plain meaning of Matthew 4:1, "Then Jesus was led up by the Spirit into the wilderness to be tempted by the devil."

What do we learn from his example that will guide us as we seek to obey the command to resist the devil?

First, we see the courage of Jesus

He did not run, nor shake in fear. I don't know what your experiences have been with evil, but there have been a few times when evil beings have been allowed (for what reason I do not know) to make themselves visible to me. At times I have been so frozen in fear that I've been unable even to speak. In one case in which I saw a demon, the mixture of immoral excess, overwhelming power, and ominous, harmful intent was so immobilizing that it was only the merciful intervention of God that saved me. Yet here is Jesus, in a humanly weak state, face to face with the evil one himself, showing no fear whatsoever.

Oh, I love Jesus! My heart swells with admiration and trust and gratitude when I see him there courageously going toe-to-toe with the very embodiment of evil. There he is, my Savior, my strong Captain, my Elder Brother, wrestling and winning fearlessly with one before whom I would so easily cower. But Jesus does not cower; he conquers!

Have confidence in Jesus, and do not let your fear control you. Yes, there may be times when fear rises up, but we can cast ourselves on Jesus and know that our fearless Savior will prevail. Having thrown yourself on him, press forward and resist the devil. Depend on the courage of Jesus and be courageous yourself. You'll be surprised by what happens, just as his disciples were: "Lord, even the demons are subject to us in your name!"[25]

Second, we see that Jesus spoke to the devil.

It is undoubtedly important that in each temptation, Jesus audibly spoke back to Satan. Finally, in verse 12, Jesus ordered him to leave. "Then Jesus said to him, 'Be gone, Satan!'"

The devil and his demons are not omniscient. They cannot read your mind. Granted, they have had thousands of years of experience with human beings and have learned a lot about human psychology and behavior. As every generation of humans dies and new generations are born, the same horde of demons continues its work, gaining experience through the centuries. They may seem like they can read our minds, but they can't. If you want to tell the devil or one of his agents to leave, you must do more than think it—you have to open your mouth and speak.

All the examples of the apostles in the book of Acts, where there was a conflict with an evil spirit, support this approach. The apostles spoke to the spirits when they resisted them. Jesus spoke to Satan and demons. That's what we do too.

There is some confusion on this point based on a misunderstanding of Jude 1:9. That verse says,

> But when the archangel Michael, contending with
> the devil, was disputing about the body of Moses,
> he did not presume to pronounce a blasphemous
> judgment, but said, "The Lord rebuke you."

I have heard it said that this verse supports the idea that we should not directly speak words of resistance to the devil. This is suggested because Michael didn't presume to pronounce something against the devil, and because Michael didn't say, "*I* rebuke you." But

---

[25] Luke 10:17.

proponents of this line of thinking have not paid sufficient attention to the details of this verse.

The issue being warned against in Jude 1:9 is not that of resisting the devil, but that of pronouncing blasphemous judgment. Michael refused to pronounce such a judgment. But what did Michael do? He resisted the devil by speaking to him and saying, "The Lord rebuke you." It is a legitimate observation that Michael did not say, "*I* rebuke you," but I would point out that he was in fact rebuking. He said, "The Lord rebuke you," but it was Michael's own mouth from which the rebuke came. He was speaking in the name and authority of the Lord, addressing the evil one. That is exactly what we do although the basis of our ability to speak in the Lord's name is different than that of the angels. Jude 1:9 supports verbally resisting the devil. Michael confronted the devil using the same principle as we use: always deal with the devil in the authority of the Lord.

Some people oppose the idea of addressing the devil based on verses like the following:

> There shall not be found among you anyone who…
> practices divination or tells fortunes or interprets
> omens, or a sorcerer or a charmer or a medium or
> a necromancer or one who inquires of the dead, for
> whoever does these things is an abomination to the
> Lord.[26]

In this passage we clearly understand that God forbids us from trying to contact and communicate with the unseen realm. But in the case of resisting the devil, we are not inquiring anything of him, nor are we seeking information from him. We are usually not even initiating the encounter—we are responding to the approach of the evil one and giving a command. It is important to understand that when resisting the devil, we are not entering a conversation *with* him; we are issuing

---

[26]   Deuteronomy 18:10 – 12.

an order *to* him. To verbally resist the devil is to obey God's command and is not a violation of verses like those found in Deuteronomy 18.

Many Christians have never done this and are intimidated by the idea of speaking out loud and ordering the devil away. They are comfortable with praying and asking God to protect them but hesitate to take the next step and address the devil. I understand that reticence, for I once felt the same way. I can only say that there are times when such a thing is necessary, and as I began to recognize those times and verbally resist the devil, I quickly experienced the work of God in pushing the enemy away from me. I honestly believe that there are times when, to successfully resist the devil, you must open your mouth and order him out.

Third, we see that in each temptation Jesus quoted Scripture.

This is a tremendously important observation. When we compare Jesus' temptation episode in the wilderness with the famous "armor of God" passage in Ephesians 6, we discern why Scripture is quoted when in conflict with the devil.

> Stand therefore, having fastened on the belt of truth, and having put on the breastplate of righteousness, and, as shoes for your feet, having put on the readiness given by the gospel of peace. In all circumstances take up the shield of faith, with which you can extinguish all the flaming darts of the evil one; and take the helmet of salvation, and the sword of the Spirit, which is the word of God.[27]

It has been observed that of all the armor mentioned only the sword is an offensive weapon. The rest of the armor is defensive. Only the sword is used to attack. In Paul's illustration the sword, of course, represents the Word of God.

---

[27] Ephesians 6:14 – 17.

When we remember our Lord's example in the wilderness temptations, we see him quoting Scripture at Satan. Three times Jesus was attacked. Three times he said, "It is written." The verses Jesus chose to use against Satan corresponded to the particular temptation with which he was faced. Each "thrust of the sword" brought an end to that attempt of the enemy.

If Jesus deliberately used the Word of God to resist the devil, then we need to do the same. Sometimes in the heat of battle I cannot think of a particular verse that relates to my present situation, so I fall back on James 4:7b. After resisting the devil, I end by saying, "For the Word of God says, 'Resist the devil and he will flee.' So, Satan, you must flee!" He backs off when a child of God stands in his or her authority and uses the Word of God.

One reason the use of Scripture is so important is that deception is always entwined with the assault. Subtly, and with great malice, the devil is continually trying to get us to believe lies and half-truths. Even when he is being cast out of a situation, he often leaves behind insinuations that sow seeds of deception. Jesus told us that the devil "has nothing to do with the truth, because there is no truth in him. When he lies, he speaks out of his own character, for he is a liar and the father of lies."[28] In confrontation with him, we need the truth to expose the falsehood of what we are being presented with, and to clear our own heads of any deception that is trying to lodge there. Quoting Scripture accomplishes all of this.

Often when we are resisting the devil, we do not have the opportunity to open the Bible and search for verses. It is the verses that we have committed to memory that we are most able to use amid the conflict. There are some verses that I have memorized precisely because they are useful in spiritual conflict. When I've been repeatedly tempted in a particular area of life, I have gone to the Bible to find verses that match the particular deception that Satan is attempting. Then after memorizing the verses, I will present

---

28   John 8:44.

them against him if the situation warrants. I always sense great power in doing this, and the temptations lessen in both frequency and strength.[29]

Resist the Devil!

Be courageous in Jesus, speak out loud to the enemy when resisting, and quote Scripture. These are three lessons for us from Jesus' example of resisting the devil in the wilderness.

Below is a sample of wording that I often use. The words themselves are not magic. Reciting them apart from personal faith in Christ and the work of the Spirit will not bring any relief. I offer this to you, however, as a helpful example. It is not aimed at any particular temptation. I offer it to you as a general way to resist the devil when needed.

Satan, in the name and authority of Jesus Christ the Lord, I rebuke you and order you away from me, for the Word of God says, "Resist the devil and he will flee from you." So, be gone! You must flee!

This kind of pointed, direct resistance is best carried out when couched in prayer. In the midst of the struggle, I will pray. I will confess my sin, claim my forgiveness, worship the Lord, and ask God for his help in the spiritual struggle in which I've found myself. Then, momentarily, I will shift my focus off God and onto Satan. I will rebuke him with words like those in the sample above, and then immediately turn my focus back to the Lord. I will continue to worship him and ask for a new filling of the Holy Spirit. Addressing the devil is only momentary, and only for the purpose of ordering him out of the situation. My enduring attention is on the Lord.

This kind of direct confrontation of the devil is not always necessary. Much of his influence on my life is indirect—it comes

---

[29] A few verses that are always helpful when resisting the devil are: James 4:7b; 2 Corinthians 10:4; 1 John 4:4b; Colossians 1:13 – 14 and Revelation 12:11.

to me via the sinful world system in which I live. Also, many of my problems are of my own doing—my sinful nature pulls me in the wrong direction. In these normal circumstances, I avail myself of all the help that the Lord gives to enable me to obey him rather than obeying my flesh or the world. There are times, however, when those normal means of the Lord's help are not enough. Be it an opening I gave the evil one by my sin, or a sudden unexpected demonic onslaught, there can be a presence of evil and its associated strength. I must rise in the name of the Lord and resist. I must speak and push the devil out of the situation.

The wonder of it all is that when I do resist in this way, I find the same result that Jesus did in the wilderness: "Then the devil left him."[30]

---

[30] Matthew 4:11.

7

ELIZABETH'S STORY

*The Lord offers to us weapons for repelling every
kind of attack. It remains for us to apply them to
use, and not leave them hanging on the wall.*
                                        John Calvin

M y wife and I received a letter from a woman who we had visited a few weeks earlier. I share it with you with her permission.

Dear Pastor and Mrs. Boone,

Thank you so much for coming to our home last month. It was a great time of encouragement for all of us.

I wanted to update you on my nightmare/sleep situation. I am thankful the Lord led me to share with you my struggles with "night terrors." I'm almost through the book you recommended to me.[31]

Several weeks ago, we experienced something that we will never forget.

You told me to rebuke Satan in the name of Jesus in the middle of these night terrors. If I'm being completely honest, I hadn't been able to address Satan directly. Now, I could do that easily in the middle of the day and have done that for my kids when I was fully awake. But when having these terrors, I would get up and pray and call out Jesus' name, but never speaking to Satan and telling him to leave in the authority of Jesus. It was too terrifying for me to speak to Satan in that state. You see, when I wake up from these terrors, the fear of someone or something ready to attack me or my family is 100% real and to address Satan—to speak directly to him or the demonic power in my home—when I'm feeling the most vulnerable, I just was too afraid to do it. I was also half out of it, in my sleep/dream world, and my semi-conscious state didn't seem to allow for that. And just to give you a picture of how my night terrors have been so real over the years, one time I kicked a hole through our bedroom door and almost broke my ankle. Another time, I elbowed a friend's mirror and injured my elbow, swelling and bruising, but thankfully not broken. Another time, I grabbed

---

31   The book she referred to is Mark Bubeck's *The Adversary.*

our daughter as a newborn from her crib and jumped into the bathtub to hide from an "attacker." Another time, running away from one of these visions, I fell down the stairs and broke my toe. I would experience traumatic events every single night.

Anyway, several Saturdays ago, my girlfriends from our former church were having a girls' night at one of their homes. The conversation turned to spiritual warfare as I shared with them my struggles, which had been increasing, and I told them all that they should read the book you had recommended. One of the girls there shared about counsel they had received years ago regarding spiritual warfare...things like rebuking Satan, burning anything like an idol or anything that was associated with Satan, confessing sins of previous generations, and so on. Another shared about her brother being possessed (Her family was involved in witchcraft when she was a child). The conversation was heavy, and my friends strongly encouraged me again to tell Satan to leave...rebuke him directly in the name of Jesus. The girls very frankly told me my position in Christ and to do it. They even suggested saying Jesus' name several times out loud first until I got the confidence to speak directly to Satan. I needed to get over it and just do it, and I think the pep talk and reading associated Scriptures gave me the confidence to engage. So, I decided that night that I would attempt this the next time it happened.

The conversation that night was very encouraging, but also rattling, as we were all reminded of the demonic realm and the real attacks of Satan in our lives. Driving home, I couldn't take the backroads through the woods because I was scared. When I got home at about 11 p.m., Jeffrey was asleep in our bed along with one of our sons next to him. I prayed and went to sleep quickly. And then I had a terrifying night terror: some black shadowy figure coming down over our sliding glass door—it was as real as they always appear. I woke up, said Jesus' name a few times and very timidly was able to rebuke Satan in Jesus' name and told him to leave. I was able to fall back asleep but woke up again shortly after with a second terrifying vision in the room. This time, I also rebuked Satan in the name of Jesus and told him to leave again. I fell back asleep more easily and didn't have any more night terrors that night. Jeffrey appeared to be asleep the whole time... he doesn't rouse easily, and frankly, he's gotten used to sleeping through my "terrors."

The next morning, Jeffrey and I went to church and were sitting in Sunday School waiting for class to start. I said to Jeffrey, "Did you hear me last night?! I rebuked Satan for the first time during my night terror!" I went on to tell him about my girls' night conversation and how excited I was that I was able to rebuke Satan. Jeffrey very soberly said that he did in fact hear me.

Jeffrey went on to tell me that when I rebuked Satan he saw a black, child-sized shadowy figure sprint from my side of the bed towards the door, and it disappeared before it went out the door. He said that he was very shaken. I asked him why he didn't tell me this sooner! He said that he wasn't sure if what he saw was real or not, but having heard that the night before my girlfriends and I had a major discussion about spiritual warfare, and that that was the first time I rebuked Satan, he knew what was going on. I also asked him if he has ever had dreams like that, thinking that maybe he was asleep. But no, he's never had a dream or anything like that. He was definitely awake. He also said he knew it wasn't one of the kids because of how the figure was moving and that it went without any sound.

It's amazing to me that the Lord allowed Jeffrey to see it. If I had seen it, I probably wouldn't have known whether I was dreaming or not. But the Lord allowed Jeffrey to see that for a reason. As soon as we got home from church, Jeffrey gathered our entire family at the doorway to our home, even insisting that our two-year-old be with us. He prayed specifically for protection over our home, our family, and against the evil one. It was a special moment.

I have had no night terrors since that night. Zero! And I was getting these every night, even several times a night. I woke up to one of the "figures" the other night (first time in over a month since the event) and I wouldn't even call it a terror because I wasn't scared. I rebuked Satan in the name of Jesus, told it to leave, and fell back asleep easily. But the fear or terror wasn't there... at all. Honestly, I believe the Lord is giving me victory over fear—even fears in other areas of my life.

Well, thanks again for the encouragement. I just had to share this with you both. I would have told you in person, but I wanted to write this down anyway, so that I'd never forget.

In Christ, Elizabeth

8

THE MEANS OF GRACE

The Christian's armor decays two ways: either by violent attack, when the Christian is overcome by temptation to sin; or else by neglecting to furbish and scour it with the use of those means which are as oil to keep it clean and bright.

William Gurnall

During my teenage years I entered a period of several months in which I was in increasing turmoil. I couldn't stop thinking about God even though I felt that something was wrong between me and him. My guilt and confusion were mounting. Finally, I wound up at a youth rally where the gospel was presented. Despite my fear of people's opinion or scorn, when the invitation to believe in Christ was given, I got up from my seat in the middle of the second-to-last row of the auditorium, clambered over people's knees to get to the aisle, and almost ran down front. God brought me to faith and I was born again.

I still remember what happened immediately after surrendering to Christ. The man who had prayed with me handed me a New Testament, looked me in the eye, and said, "Read this every day."

He didn't use the phrase *means of grace*, but that is what he was talking about. I needed to get into reading that Bible, so that God would use it to pour grace into my life.

I soon realized that prayer and fellowship would also be used of God to help me grow. I needed to be committed to them as well as to the Bible. In those days I did not hear anyone call Bible reading, prayer, and fellowship *means of grace*, but people did teach me that my growth depended, in part, upon my faithfulness in participating in those three activities.

Those early months of my Christian life are now over forty years in the past. During those years I've struggled with temptation and sin, wrestled with understanding the difference between my part and God's part in my growth, experienced victories from the Lord's hand, and rejoiced in the progress that God has worked in me. I'm still growing, but at least now I know what I am to do in order to keep growing. And "what I am to do" involves *the means of grace*.

Nothing that I have shared with you about resisting the devil replaces the importance of involving yourself in the means of grace. As a matter of fact, a consistent use of the means of grace is the way we prevent many of the devil's attacks. It is *preventative resistance*.

I'd like to share with you what I've learned about the means of grace, and I do so with the prayer that you will be helped in your own spiritual growth.

It is a relationship.

I want to say right here at the start—I am talking about a relationship with the living Jesus Christ. If you miss this fact, then what I am going to share with you will be a burden to perform, or perhaps one more "Christian" approach to self-help. If you have been born again, however, you have left religion behind and embraced personal reconciliation with God. You do not merely know about him; you know *him*. Don't let Satan use the discussion about the means of grace to push you towards viewing Christianity as a system of activities to accomplish. Real Christianity is a relationship.

Grace is two-fold.

I have found over the years that many Christians who have attended church services for decades are still not aware that there are two main parts to God's grace.

The first is God's merciful arrangement for our forgiveness. "For by grace you have been saved through faith; and that not of yourselves, it is the gift of God."[32] This is the aspect of God's grace that normally comes to mind first when we are asked, "What is grace?" We receive forgiveness, not because we deserve it, but because God graciously gives it.

Grace:
① means forgiveness of sin

After we receive forgiveness, however, grace is still operating in us. Grace does not merely get us saved; it then causes us to grow. This second part of God's grace is meant to be our daily experience. We define this second part of grace as the divine enablement to obey him. It is the infusing of his strength into us, enabling us to engage our will and assume our responsibilities in following him. It is personal and experiential. "You therefore, my son, be strong in the grace that is in Christ Jesus."[33]

② Enablement to follow / obey Christ

God's grace is: (1) his merciful arrangement for our forgiveness; and (2) his enablement of us to obey.

We can see both parts of God's grace in Hebrews 4:16. "Therefore let us draw near with confidence to the throne of grace, so that we may receive mercy [*the first part*] and find grace to help [*the second part*] in time of need."

The second aspect of God's grace is what we spiritually live off of every day. It is the ability to think, speak, and act as we ought and to refuse to think, speak, and act as we ought not. That grace is

---

[32] Ephesians 2:8.
[33] 2 Timothy 2:1.

given to us by the Holy Spirit—but it is not necessarily automatic. He normally gives that grace to us via *means*.

The other day I had to do some home repairs. Among other tasks, I had to remove several bolts that were tightened into place. I got the bolts unfastened—but not with my bare hands. I used a wrench. The wrench was the *means* by which I loosened and removed the bolts. There are means by which God the Spirit pours grace into our lives, and we call them *the means of grace*.

The means are not magical.

Protestants are not the only ones who use the phrase *the means of grace*. The Roman Catholic Church does so too, but with a different meaning. In some Roman Catholic writings, and in some Protestants' minds as well, there is the idea that whatever God designates as a means of grace will convey grace to us merely by our choosing to use it. We could almost use the word "magic" to describe this view. If you read the Bible, pray, etc., those things "magically" transfer God's grace to you.

I will let J. Oliver Buswell, a trusted Bible scholar, comment on this view. "There has been much discussion over the phrase, 'the means of grace,' as though evangelical... theologians were guilty of teaching that the grace of God is conveyed by some outward formal act, as an act in itself. The phrase used by Roman Catholic authorities to express their view that the sacraments are the means of grace is '*ex opera operato*.' That is to say, by the outward physical act of the doing of the particular work, the blessing is conveyed. Protestant authorities vigorously deny any such doctrine."[34]

Let me put Buswell's thoughts into my own words. Taking the Lord's Supper, for example, does not magically or automatically transfer God's grace to you. Reading the Bible does not magically transfer grace to you. The means of grace are for us to participate in,

---

34   J. Oliver Buswell, *A Systematic Theology of the Christian Religion* (Singapore: Christian Life Publishers PTE LTD, 1994), 227.

but it is the person of the Holy Spirit who gives grace or who does not. Remember, we are talking about a relationship with God—not a set of religious practices. So, we do *not* believe that there is some inert spiritual power in the means of grace that operates apart from the intention and action of God the Spirit.

That is why we look to God as we avail ourselves of the means of grace. We are careful to use the means, but our focus is on God rather than on the means. An English pastor in the 1600's, William Secker, said it well, "Neither be idle in the means, nor make an idol of the means."

Consider this question.

Before listing the means of grace, I want you to think carefully about a crucial question: who causes you to grow spiritually? Your answer to that question will shape how you approach your Christian life. If, either deliberately or without consciously realizing it, you have come to believe that *you* cause your growth, you will labor to conform to certain standards, attitudes and activities. Lasting peace and a sense of freedom will always elude you. If, on the other hand, you are convinced that it is *God* who causes your growth, you will have an entirely different experience.

Scripture teaches us that it is indeed God who causes our spiritual maturity. The Apostle Paul said, "I planted, Apollos watered, but God gave the growth. So neither he who plants nor he who waters is anything, but only God who gives the growth."[35] Twice in that short passage Paul makes the point that it is God who causes spiritual growth. Paul even contrasts himself and another church leader with God. Neither Paul nor Apollos produced spiritual progress in the Corinthian Christians—it was God who did that.

---

[35]   1 Corinthians 3:6 – 7.

It is true that we bear some responsibility for our progress in Christian maturity, just as Paul and Apollos were responsible to plant and water, but we must not conclude that because we are partly responsible, we are therefore able to make ourselves grow. Please understand this point: The source of our spiritual growth is God.

God causes our growth, and uses means to do so.

This spiritual progress that God produces in us is a result of grace. The gracious work of his Spirit changes us, matures us, sanctifies us. In that work, he uses means. He has shown us in his word what those means are. When we participate in those means, the Spirit often uses them to pour grace into our lives, thereby causing us to grow.

So, what are the means of grace?

What are the means of grace? I've mentioned a few of them already, but is there a comprehensive list? Interestingly enough, there is a wide variance among theologians as to what belongs on that list. Louis Berkhof lists only the preached Word, the Lord's Supper, and baptism.[36] Charles Hodge adds prayer to that list.[37] Wayne Grudem expands the list to include eleven items: teaching of the Word, baptism, the Lord's Supper, prayer for one another, worship, church discipline, giving, spiritual gifts, fellowship, evangelism, personal ministry to individuals.[38]

I've developed a basic version of the means of grace. My list has eight foundational means. They can be remembered in this way: 1 – 2 – 3 – ! One = one external thing. Two = two internal attitudes. Three = three activities. The exclamation mark = Don't forget the ordinances!

---

[36]   Louis Berkhof, *Systematic Theology* (Grand Rapids: Eerdmans Publishing, 1981) 604.

[37]   Alan Cairns, *Dictionary of Theological Terms* (Greenville: Ambassador Emerald International, 2002) 274 – 275.

[38]   Wayne Grudem, *Systematic Theology* (Grand Rapids: Zondervan, 1994) 951.

1 = One External Thing

The Word of God. God uses his Word to pour grace into our lives and change us. This can occur in all of the ways in which we interact with the Word—listening to it being read, hearing it preached and taught, reading it ourselves, memorizing it, praying from it, studying it.

The Apostle Peter expressed it this way, "Like newborn babies, long for the pure milk of the word, so that by it you may grow in respect to salvation."[39] God uses his Word in our lives to cause us to grow.

This particular means of grace is especially important in light of the devil's tactics. He constantly works to deceive us. A steady diet of the truth makes us less susceptible to our enemy's lies. You may not have thought of your daily devotions in this light, but as you get into the Word of God, you are in fact protecting yourself from the devil.

2 = Two Internal Attitudes

Two attitudes are crucial for growth to occur. I must admit that internal attitudes are not listed in the traditional discussion of the means of grace. Nevertheless, I see in them a similar importance and dynamic concerning our Christian maturity, and so I include them on my list. The two attitudes are Trust and Obedience.

Trust (or Faith) is crucial for our growth. Look at the importance faith is given in relation to spiritual profit. "For indeed we have had good news preached to us, just as they also; but the word they heard did not profit them, because it was not united by faith in those who heard."[40] Where faith was present, there was spiritual benefit. Where faith was absent, even the presence of the Word of God brought no growth.

A few years ago I was going through a deep trial, a protracted time of physical suffering that was bringing me face-to-face with the

---

[39] 1 Peter 2:2.

[40] Hebrews 4:2.

possibility of losing my ability to work. I was very worried about my future and my family. One evening I was sitting in a chair at my house with the Bible open on my lap. As I read a psalm, I trusted. I trusted God for all that was worrying me, and peace overwhelmed me. I rose from the chair and faced the exact same problems, but with new strength. God had filled me with grace. Nothing had changed except my internal attitude—I had trusted God, and his grace was flowing.

Obedience (or Submission) is also crucial for our growth. Jesus said, "Whoever has my commandments and keeps them, he it is who loves me. And he who loves me will be loved by my Father, and I will love him and manifest myself to him."[41] It is not enough to have Jesus' words; we must obey them. When we resist God's movement in our lives, the flow of grace stops. When we surrender to his will, the grace flows. Perhaps this is partly why our Lord taught us to pray, "Your will be done on earth as it is in heaven." Submission opens the flow of grace.

The 19th Century songwriter John Sammis got it right in the chorus of his famous hymn. "Trust and obey, for there's no other way, to be happy in Jesus, but to trust and obey."

3 = Three Activities

In addition to the Word of God, Trust, and Obedience, there are three activities that God uses to pour grace into us as we participate in them.

Prayer. We pray alone and we pray with other Christians. We pray silently and we pray out loud. We pray in various settings, in different postures, and at various times. But in every case as we pray, the Spirit of God can use that experience to pour grace into our lives. Jesus presented prayer as a crucial part of our progress in discipleship. "If you abide in me, and my words abide in you, ask whatever you wish, and it will be done for you. By this my Father is glorified, that

---

[41]   John 14:21.

you bear much fruit and so prove to be my disciples."[42] The Apostle Paul believed that the experience of grace was linked to prayer. "For this reason I bow my knees before the Father…that he may grant you to be strengthened with power through his Spirit in your inner being."[43] Prayer is a means of grace.

Fellowship. The Apostle Paul stresses that the spiritual growth we experience is linked strongly to our participation in the lives of our fellow Christians. "Christ…from whom the whole body, being fitted and held together by what every joint supplies, according to the proper working of each individual part, causes the growth of the body for the building up of itself in love."[44]

As we involve ourselves in each other's lives, the Spirit inhabits that fellowship and pours grace into us. Fellowship is a means of grace.

Service. I've underlined a few spots in the following Scripture to draw attention to the fact that our service is a means that God uses to help us grow.

> And He gave some as apostles, and some as prophets, and some as evangelists, and some as pastors and teachers, for the equipping of the saints for the work of service, to the building up of the body of Christ; until we all attain to the unity of the faith, and of the knowledge of the Son of God, to a mature man, to the measure of the stature which belongs to the fullness of Christ.[45]

As we serve, grace flows and gives us progress in spiritual maturity. God gives grace to others through our service, but he also gives grace to us. We grow by serving.

---

[42] John 15:7 – 8.

[43] Ephesians 3:14 – 16.

[44] Ephesians 4:15 – 16.

[45] Ephesians 4:11 – 13.

! = Don't Forget the Ordinances

There are two ordinances of the church, both of which were given to us by the Lord and deserve our special attention.[46] Woe to us if we avoid or underestimate them. Blessed are we if we participate in them.

Baptism. Paul speaks about our baptism in a way that shows the seriousness with which we ought to consider it. "Do you not know that all of us who have been baptized into Christ Jesus were baptized into his death? We were buried therefore with him by baptism into death, in order that, just as Christ was raised from the dead by the glory of the Father, we too might walk in newness of life."[47] There is a link between the newness of our life—the personal transformation we undergo—and our baptism. Baptism is a means of grace.

The Lord's Supper. Although there has been much controversy among professing Christians over the precise meaning of the Lord's Supper, I think we can agree that the following verse teaches us that something special takes place in it. "Is not the cup of blessing which we bless a sharing in the blood of Christ? Is not the bread which we break a sharing in the body of Christ?"[48] God uses the Lord's Table to heighten our communion with Him. The Lord's Supper is a means of grace.

1 – 2 – 3 – !

One external thing: The Word of God.

Two internal attitudes: Trust and Obey.

Three activities: Prayer, Fellowship, and Service.

And the ordinances: Baptism and The Lord's Supper.

As we avail ourselves of these means, the sovereign Spirit of God uses them to pour grace into our lives and cause spiritual growth. The enemy of our souls is on the prowl, and the ones who participate

---

[46]   Some churches refer to these as sacraments.

[47]   Romans 6:3 – 4.

[48]   1 Corinthians 10:16.

in these means in their daily and weekly routines are ensuring that the posture of their lives is one in which Satan has little advantage. For the sake of defending yourself from the devil, and for the sake of your spiritual maturity, commit yourself to the means of grace.

Means of Transformation ?
→ Likely to contain many of the above means of grace ... also might include:
* Trials ; suffering
* Church discipline
* practices of contentment
*

9

ALL THREE SOURCES OF OUR TROUBLE

Our corrupted hearts are the factories of the devil, which may be at work without his presence; for when that scheming spirit has drawn malice, envy, and all unrighteousness into well-rooted habits in his disciples, iniquity then goes upon its own legs.

Sir Thomas Browne

Christians are used to the idea that there is a trio of sources from which the conflicts of our lives come: the world, the flesh, and the devil. Identifying the origin of our troubles in this way is helpful and biblical.

The world: We live in a godless society that is full of unredeemed men and women whose values and decisions are driven by their lusts, greed, and pride.[49] Their concerted energy and godless intentions coalesce into systems, power structures, and pervasive beliefs and

---

[49]   1 John 2:16.

attitudes that are enormously influential on anyone living in their culture. We all live in such a society, and have been warned not to "love the world or the things in the world."[50]

The flesh: Our sin nature is not taken away from us until we are glorified in heaven.[51] Although our guilt is gone when we believe in Christ, our inner propensity to sin is not. Our sin nature is like gravity—it is always present and always pulling us down. Romans 6 – 8 teaches us that when we reckon our status with God to be what he himself says it is (i.e., that we have died and risen with Christ), then the door is open for us to receive the help of the Holy Spirit and to put a cap on our sinful nature. Our wrongful inclinations are still present, but we are no longer obligated to follow them. We can experience the freedom to obey God rather than our flesh.

Our flesh is an extremely potent source of downfall. James described our temptations this way:

> Let no one say when he is tempted, "I am being tempted by God," for God cannot be tempted with evil, and he himself tempts no one. But each person is tempted when he is lured and enticed by his own desire. Then desire when it has conceived gives birth to sin, and sin when it is fully grown brings forth death.[52]

The latent desires within us enable temptations coming from the outside to be effective. We are warned not to let sin reign in our bodies, and not to obey our sin nature's passions.[53]

The devil: The devil contributes to the blindness, corruption, and unholy momentum of the world. He also capitalizes on the

---

50   1 John 2:15.
51   1 John 3:2.
52   James 1:13 – 15.
53   Romans 6:12; 8:13.

weaknesses of our flesh, aiming at sinful desires within us while attempting to create a foothold.

The devil is not, however, directly involved in *every* temptation. He does not need to be directly involved since the combination of our own flesh and the world system is so strong. The devil exerts much of his influence on us indirectly. He fans the flames of deception, sensuality, religious evil, relationship problems, indulgence, and covetousness, which are in the world. The world then pulls us towards sin in each of those areas. When we succumb, it is not always because the devil or a demon was present at the time of temptation. Rather, it is often because we capitulated in the face of the combination of our own flesh and the world.

I have seen some Christians, with lives in disarray, come to pastors for help and yet resist the requirements that godly counsel lays before them. During the process of counseling, they eagerly grab hold of the idea that Satan is involved in their situation. In my early years I was encouraged by this, but now I proceed with caution. There is a kind of false spirituality that gravitates to resisting the devil while remaining passive in the participation in the means of grace. The normal daily and weekly routines for receiving help from God are traded in for the supposed "quick fix" of resisting the devil. The disarray of their life is blamed totally on the devil, and their own responsibility is disregarded. Needless to say, as long as they proceed with this mindset, the disarray continues, and the freedom of Christ remains elusive to them.

over-blaming the devil

Our life has three sources of trouble—the world, the flesh and the devil. All three are a part of our temptations and struggles. All three must be acknowledged and responded to accordingly. In this book I am focusing on the matter of resisting the devil because it has been so under-taught, but I am in no way suggesting that what we already know about overcoming the world and the flesh is superseded by this teaching. We need to be equipped to handle all three of our problem sources and to be appropriately engaged with God against them all.

Having said that, I must admit that it is my observation that most of the Christian counseling that we give and receive has very little in it about our enemy and his schemes. Why do pastors and Christian counselors coach people so well to deal with their flesh and with the world but leave them helpless in the case of actual demonic involvement? Our silence on this issue is harming the people who come to us for help.

Just as pastors need to include the reality and power of the unseen realm in their counseling, we all need to realize that it is a part of our Christian life. We do not need to be afraid nor to be searching for demons in every situation, but we do need to be aware of the possibility of an unseen element and be ready to deal with it.

Again, many troubles come our way apart from any direct involvement, but some troubles are indeed coupled with an evil presence and the corresponding extra strength that comes with such a presence. When we suspect an evil one's personal presence, we rebuke it so as to eliminate it from the situation. Then we are left with our flesh and the world with which we then deal as Scripture instructs us.

How do you tell if a temptation is combined with a direct attack by the devil? I don't know of any formula that gives an easy answer to that question. Discernment comes as you lean on the Holy Spirit who indwells you. In prayer, you ask God for help. If you are doing everything you know to do, and the spiritual assault is still strong, and you can't seem to shake it off, then I would suspect a demonic element. There are times, too, when there is a force to the temptation that is beyond normal. That is also the time to claim your authority in Christ and order the evil one to depart.

[margin note: knowing whether the devil is involved or not?]

There are occasions when I am not sure, and in those cases I open my mouth and resist the devil anyway. If there is no evil presence, I have done no harm. If there indeed was an evil presence, then it is driven out. But in most cases in which I verbally resist the devil, I have some sense that there is an attack of an evil one that must be pointedly resisted.

The world, the flesh and the devil—all three are foisting spiritual harm upon us. We must deal with all three. But again, we deal with them not as those who are trying to establish the initial victory, but as those who are standing in the victory that has been already won! Jesus said, "But take heart; I have overcome the world." The Apostle Paul tells us that because we are in Christ's death and resurrection, the flesh is defeated. "We know that our old self was crucified with him in order that the body of sin might be brought to nothing, so that we would no longer be enslaved to sin." The writer of Hebrews tells us that by his death, Christ defeated the devil. "Since therefore the children share in flesh and blood, he himself likewise partook of the same things, that through death he might destroy the one who has the power of death, that is, the devil."[54] Our Savior has defeated all three!

How I praise the Lord Jesus! He has defeated all our enemies. The world, flesh, and devil are all undone by him. Although the victory is established, it is not yet consummated. We live with the cross behind us and the utter demise of Satan still before us. So there is wrestling that we do, but we do it in Christ and his already-accomplished victory. The exhortation to "be strong in the Lord and in the strength of his might"[55] means increasingly more to us as we understand our enemies and what Christ has done to them. May the Lord Jesus be praised for his great victory and for his willingness to share it with us!

"In your hand are power and might, and in your hand it is to make great and to give strength to all. And now we thank you, our God, and praise your glorious name!"[56]

---

[54]   John 16:33; Romans 6:6; Hebrews 2:14.

[55]   Ephesians 6:10.

[56]   1 Chronicles 29:12 – 13.

10

LESSONS FROM JOB

A child of God never more triumphs than in his greatest troubles.

Richard Sibbes

Job is one of my favorite books of the Bible, but that wasn't always the case. For most of my life, I avoided the book of Job because I found it to be so confusing. Then there came a time in my life when God allowed me to go through a prolonged period of intense suffering, which propelled me into the Scriptures to search for help. In that search I wound up in the book of Job, and what I found there brought lasting comfort and gave me increased confidence in the Lord. I cannot write here all that I learned in Job—that would take another book—but I would like to share with you five important lessons that I found in Job that help us as we wrestle with the devil.[57]

---

[57] It would be helpful if you take the time now to read the first two chapters of Job.

Lesson #1: Satan only does what God allows.

In the first two chapters of Job, we are given a unique glimpse into the heavens and what we see surprises us—Satan gets an audience with the Lord. We pick up the story after God has drawn Satan's attention to Job.

> Then Satan answered the Lord and said, "Does Job fear God for no reason? Have you not put a hedge around him and his house and all that he has, on every side? You have blessed the work of his hands, and his possessions have increased in the land. But stretch out your hand and touch all that he has, and he will curse you to your face." And the Lord said to Satan, "Behold, all that he has is in your hand. Only against him do not stretch out your hand." So Satan went out from the presence of the Lord.[58]

Prior to this conversation God had "drawn a circle in the sand" around Job, his family, and his work enterprises, and told Satan that he couldn't cross the line. Then God erases that circle and draws a smaller one closer to Job. "Behold, all that he has is in your hand. Only against him do not stretch out your hand."[59]

We shudder as the account continues. Satan works his destruction on Job's property and even on his children. Job does not cease to worship God, however, and this fact is pointed out to Satan by God. Then Satan responds,

> "Skin for skin! All that a man has he will give for his life. But stretch out your hand and touch his bone and his flesh, and he will curse you to your face." And the Lord said to Satan, "Behold, he is in your hand; only spare his life."[60]

---

[58]   Job 1:9 – 12.

[59]   Job 1:12.

[60]   Job 2:4 – 6.

Now God erases the second line and draws a third smaller circle even closer to Job. God allows Satan to inflict harm on Job's body but not to kill him.

Satan never attacks us without God's permission. There is great mystery involved in this truth. It strikes at one of humanity's great questions: Why has God allowed evil in this world? The book of Job addresses that question, but let's not rush to that issue without thinking further about God's sovereignty. Evil is present in our world and experience, but it is not outside of God's control. The fact that it is under his control does not mean, however, that he is morally responsible for it. He allows evil. He even uses evil. But he is not culpable for evil.

I love the way the book of Habakkuk shows us this truth. At the risk of oversimplifying that prophet's book, let me summarize it this way:

Habakkuk: "God, your people are sinning against you. How long will you do nothing about this?"

God: "I'm sending the Chaldeans to punish my people."

Habakkuk: "The Chaldeans?! They are evil people! They are worse than we are. How can you do that?!"

God: "Oh, I will hold them responsible for what they are going to do to you. I will punish them."

At this point we are scratching our heads in confusion. The Lord says that he will use the Chaldeans, and then punish them for the very thing he used them to do. Habakkuk was scratching his head too, but his eventual response is one of the great take-aways from his prophecy.

> Though the fig tree should not blossom, nor fruit be on the vines, the produce of the olive fail and the fields yield no food, the flock be cut off from the fold and there be no herd in the stalls, yet I will rejoice in the Lord; I will take joy in the God of my salvation. God, the Lord, is my strength; he makes

my feet like the deer's; he makes me tread on my
high places.[61]

Habakkuk's eventual response was worship. That was also Job's
response to his suffering. "Then Job arose and tore his robe and
shaved his head and fell on the ground and worshiped."[62] That is
also what our fundamental response ought to be when we are the
target of the devil's malice. An attack from the evil one does not
mean that something has slipped by God and touched us un-noticed
by him. Suffering in which the devil has a hand is not evidence that
God's power is limited but a sign that our sovereign God is up to
something. We worship him throughout the test and remember that
whatever is testing us has come with his permission.

Let me take this one step further. We are instructed to "give
thanks in all circumstances; for this is the will of God in Christ Jesus
for you."[63] I suggest that satanic attacks are included in that verse's
little word "all." There is something deeply good and God-honoring
when one of his children is in the midst of a painful spiritual struggle,
and yet he or she bows down and thanks God for the struggle. We are
not thanking him for the evil—but for his sovereignty in allowing it
and for his purposes (even though we cannot always see them.)

Many Christians testify that direct conflict with the devil, although
at first very frightening, has brought them into a deeper understanding
of their place in Christ, has intensified their personal experience of
depending on the Lord, has resulted in greater personal holiness, and
brought more joy. There may have been other hidden purposes in the
mind of God for allowing such attacks, but those consequences are
certainly reason to praise Him. Christians who allow God to use them
in resisting the devil wind up like Job and Habakkuk—worshiping
intensely, and experiencing more joy and strength.

---

[61]   Habakkuk 3:17 – 19.
[62]   Job 1:20.
[63]   1 Thessalonians 5:18.

Lesson #2: Satan can severely hurt us at times.

It is impossible to read the first two chapters of Job without recoiling. Job was hurt, and hurt deeply. How can we overstate how grievously he suffered? His means of income was destroyed. His property was taken. His children were killed. And finally, his body was racked with pain.

The book is full of Job's cries of anguish. "Why did I not die at birth?" "My face is red with weeping." "Look at me and be appalled." [64] His suffering was real, it was severe, and it was all provoked by Satan. Satan can indeed hurt us.

But what about the promises of God's protection? For example, in Psalm 121 we see the child of God's confidence in the protection of the Lord.

> I lift up my eyes to the hills. From where does my help come? My help comes from the Lord, who made heaven and earth. He will not let your foot be moved; he who keeps you will not slumber. Behold, he who keeps Israel will neither slumber nor sleep. The Lord is your keeper; the Lord is your shade on your right hand. The sun shall not strike you by day, nor the moon by night. The Lord will keep you from all evil; he will keep your life. The Lord will keep your going out and your coming in from this time forth and forevermore. [65]

How do we balance the clear expression of God's intent to protect us with the equally clear example that Satan can at times inflict great harm on us? The answer is in the mind of God, and in the nature of our in-between existence. He alone knows when it serves his purposes to allow what he normally would not allow. In those cases he removes his protection, but always for a purpose and

HARM ?

---

[64] Job 1:11; 16:16; 21:5.
[65] Psalm 121:1 – 8.

always with limits. We must also remember that we do not live in the Garden of Eden anymore, and we are not in heaven yet. This in-between existence is in fact a battleground. As much as you or I would wish it were otherwise, when we believed in Jesus Christ, we were drafted into God's army and placed into a combat zone. Sometimes soldiers get wounded even when the battle is won.

Think of the prayer that Jesus taught his disciples. After worship, submission, and petition, he ends with, "And lead us not into temptation, but deliver us from evil."[66] In the very pattern that our Lord gives for our prayers, we see the reality of our spiritual conflict and the need to be alert to it. Also, we remember our Lord's prayer for his disciples the night he was betrayed. "I do not ask that you take them out of the world, but that you keep them from the evil one."[67] He did not waver in his request for protection. He did not doubt the Father's heart. Neither should we.

In the midst of conflict with the evil one, we are to pray in faith. We believe God's promises and persevere in the conflict. If in a particular case we experience prolonged opposition and suffering, we rest in God, as Job eventually did, and trust in his wisdom. If there is a purpose for God allowing a certain affliction to remain in our lives, perhaps he will show it to us as he did to the Apostle Paul when he experienced a physical affliction from Satan.[68] If he doesn't, then we worship him anyway, and keep obeying his command to resist.

Lessons #3: We can suffer attacks of the evil one that are not our fault.

A few times while I was studying the book of Job in preparation for teaching it to our church, people asked me, "What is the one overarching lesson in the book?" I hesitated to answer them. I couldn't put the teaching of Job in one simple proposition. There

---

66   Matthew 6:13.
67   John 17:15.
68   2 Corinthians 12:7 – 9.

are several important lessons in Job. But one of the main lessons is this: <u>sometimes our suffering is not our fault</u>.

This is one of the sticking points between Job and his friends. They kept insisting that his suffering was in some way deserved. Job protested and asserted that, although he was not sinless, this suffering was in no way linked to any sin or shortcoming in his life. Job was correct, and in his story we learn this important lesson.

As I have already explained, it is possible for us to give a place to the devil in our lives. Through indulgence in sin or prolonged passivity, the door to our lives can be left open, and "the devil never passes an open door." On the other hand, we can be attacked through no fault of our own.

Numerous times I have talked with adults who suffered demonic attacks that originated in their parents' involvement in the occult. I know of others who have suffered a traumatic experience, and somehow the evil one gained ground in their lives through it. As *Elizabeth's Story* (chapter 7) illustrates, an attack can also be experienced by people who are otherwise walking with God. Sometimes, like Job, we are not aware of all the reasons behind the attack; all we know is that we are unexpectedly facing an onslaught of the evil one through no fault of our own.

This truth is important because <u>our accuser will attempt to make us feel guilty when there is no reason for it</u>. That is what was happening through the middle chapters of the book of Job. Through Job's friends, Satan was pouring on the pressure, trying to make Job confess to sin that wasn't his. But Satan didn't get the victory in Job's life, and he doesn't have to get the victory in ours either.

Lesson #4: We do not get all of our questions answered.

Any reader of the book of Job immediately gets more information than Job himself received. You and I know about the conversations in heaven between God and Satan, but Job never did. He went through his trial in ignorance of God's purposes. Indeed, much of the difficulty Job experienced was heightened because he did not understand why God was doing what he was doing.

But even if Job had seen what you and I see in chapters 1 – 2, it wouldn't have answered all his questions. For decades after my conversion, I looked for an answer in the Scriptures to the age-old question, "Why is there evil in the world?" I didn't see the answer, but I figured that it was there in the Bible somewhere. I just hadn't discerned it yet.

In pondering this question I discovered three common answers. (1) Evil exists because of the sinful choice of human beings. (2) God overrules evil and uses it for good. And (3) God gets glory in overcoming evil. I came to realize that those were not actually answers to the question of *why*? It is true that sinful men and women make wrong decisions, and those decisions result in more suffering, but that doesn't explain why evil is present. The serpent was present before Adam and Eve's first rebellious decision. It is also true that God uses evil for his purposes; that he overrules it, and even that he gets glory in doing so. But again, that doesn't tell us *why* evil exists in the first place. God hates evil, is thoroughly opposed to it, and has promised to destroy it. Why then has he allowed it?

Looking back over my life, I realized that there was always a nagging sense of incompleteness as I faced trials of various kinds. I would seek help in the passages in Scripture that counsel us in times of testing, and certainly God strengthened me through them. But all the while, I was living with this idea that there was an answer in the Scripture that I hadn't seen. If I could just find that answer, I would be able to make my way through life's difficulties in a more Christian way. Why does evil exist?

It took a particularly intense and prolonged trial that plunged me into suffering, which in some ways paralleled Job's, to open my eyes to what was being said in Scripture. I still remember the sense of surprise, relief, and peace that overcame me when, while immersed in the book of Job, I saw the answer to the question. Why does evil exist? The answer is: God doesn't tell us the answer.

Find peace in God's Sovereignty

He purposefully does not tell us the answer. <u>Our peace increases when we submit to God's wisdom and rest in him.</u> The point is to seek God himself rather than seeking the answer, and to rest in him without knowing the answer.

We aren't supposed to know the reason for evil's existence. As a matter of fact, we couldn't grasp the explanation even if God gave it to us. This is one of the wonderful lessons from the "nature walk" that God gives Job in chapters 38 – 39. He points Job's attention to the stars, the sky, the weather, and the animals—always punctuating this tour with questions that reveal Job's ignorance and powerlessness. I especially enjoy God's momentary focus on the ostrich.[69] Here, it is as if God is saying, "Explain that to me, Job, a bird who cannot fly but can outrun a horse!" If Job cannot explain an ostrich, he cannot understand God's explanation of why he has allowed evil.

Finally, Job ceases to ask God for explanations.

> Then Job answered the Lord and said: "I know that you can do all things, and that no purpose of yours can be thwarted...Therefore I have uttered what I did not understand, things too wonderful for me, which I did not know."[70]

The great transformation that occurred in Job was that he realized that the answers he was seeking from the Lord were "too wonderful" for him. Another translation puts it, "too difficult for me." But he also realized that God could do all things and that none of his purposes would be frustrated by evil. That was enough for Job. He would rest in God even without all the answers.

I dwell on this lesson from Job while discussing our spiritual struggle with the devil because the heart transformation that Job, I, and many others went through is important. This heart

---

[69]   Job 39:13 – 18.

[70]   Job 42:1 – 3.

transformation leaves us with a focus on God himself. If we have God, then we have enough. During the devil's attacks, life can get unpleasant. In prolonged attacks, or ones that leave lasting repercussions, we find ourselves in circumstances that we did not choose and do not want. The *why* question, if dwelt upon, distracts us from the foundation upon which we rest and fight. The foundation is God himself. Like Job, we must submit, worship, and confidently rest in the Lord.

submit,
worship,
rest in
the Lord.

A Word of Caution

I would like to use this lesson from Job as a springboard to address a reality that we encounter as we resist the devil. We often run into unknowns when engaged in spiritual conflict. That is okay, for it is the nature of this realm. We are not instructed to seek the answers to those unknowns, just to resist the devil, and then get on with life.

Questions like the following can come to mind: Why are some demons more difficult to push away than others? How is it exactly happening that the devil gets a "place" in a person's life but isn't possessing that person? Why is it that I seem to be more susceptible to the devil's attacks when I am asleep and dreaming? How can the devil put thoughts in a person's mind? What is the interaction between good angels and demons? It seems that some evil spirits are associated with places, or physical objects—how does that happen? It seems from some verses that there may be some sort of hierarchy in the demonic realm—how does that work?

It is in light of these and other questions like them that we recall prohibitions like those in Deuteronomy 18:10 – 12, which forbid us from trying to reach into the unseen realm and find out information.[71] In my experience, especially when called on to

---

71   Deuteronomy 18:10 – 12 "There shall not be found among you anyone who burns his son or his daughter as an offering, anyone who practices divination or tells fortunes or interprets omens, or a sorcerer or a charmer or a medium or a necromancer or one who inquires of the dead, for

confront a person who is clearly oppressed by the evil one, there is usually a fogginess involved in the whole process. I do not see everything clearly. Undoubtedly part of this is due to my own limitations, and part to the deceit of the enemy, but I have also come to realize that this lack of clarity is part of the nature of dealing with the unseen realm. I try not to entertain my own curiosity but to stick to what God has directed me to do: Resist the devil!

Lesson #5: A time is coming when Satan will be silenced.

Many people who have read the book of Job are surprised when they make the observation that Satan is never mentioned after the second chapter. Why, after having such an important part at the beginning of the story, would he never be referred to again? For some years I was among those who thought this way, but I eventually realized that we were all wrong. We missed it. Satan does indeed show up again, but under a different name.[72]

Following the "nature walk" of chapters 38 – 39, God moves the discussion from the natural realm to the moral. We see this in his strong words to Job in 40:6 – 14. He challenges Job to "look on everyone who is proud and bring him low and tread down the wicked where they stand."[73] In earlier chapters he had challenged Job as to his ignorance and lack of power in the natural realm. Now he calls on Job to execute universal justice. Job cannot. He is as impotent in the moral realm as in the natural.

God then introduces Behemoth.[74] The Hebrew word *behemoth* is the plural of the word for "beast." It is a plural word used in reference to a single reality, and thus we begin to get the idea that there is a symbolic meaning intended here. The creature is described as having no fear and being impossible to capture. That description

---

whoever does these things is an abomination to the Lord. And because of these abominations the Lord your God is driving them out before you."

[72] At this point it would be helpful for you to read Job 40 – 41.

[73] Job 40:12.

[74] Job 40:15 – 24.

does not fit a hippopotamus or an elephant, two animals that are regularly suggested as the "behemoth" of these chapters. As we continue from chapter 40 into 41, we conclude that this is no mere animal. It seems that God is beginning with the natural world but is taking us somewhere else. To what is God pointing our attention?

I believe that these characteristics of fearlessness and invincibility are then included and amplified with the next creature, Leviathan. "Behold, the hope of man is false; he is laid low even at the sight of him."[75] Leviathan is truly invincible. Therefore, it cannot be a mere animal. Rather, it is the personification of fearsome, malicious power. Other Scriptural references to Leviathan, or a great dragon, confirm this interpretation. Leviathan is powerful evil, which is leading the world astray, intent on opposing the purposes of God.[76] Leviathan is Satan.

The culminating truth of chapter 41 is placed near the middle of the chapter. It serves as a sort of hinge around which the rest of the chapter swings. God is making a crucial point that we must not miss.

> Who then is able to stand against me? Who has a claim against me that I must pay? Everything under heaven belongs to me. Will I not silence his [i.e., Leviathan] boastings?[77]

God is saying that everything, including evil, is under his control, and that there will come a day when the fearsome Leviathan will be silenced.

Hallelujah! Amid the evil one's attacks, we draw strength from the truth that his demise is sure.

---

[75]   Job 41:9.

[76]   Psalm 74:13 – 14; Revelation 12.

[77]   Job 41:10b – 12a. Verse 12 is very difficult to translate into English, and it is likely that your version of the Bible has different wording. In my opinion, this is the best translation.

And the devil, who deceived them, was thrown into the lake of burning sulfur, where the beast and the false prophet had been thrown. They will be tormented day and night for ever and ever.[78]

And we draw strength from the truth that our complete deliverance is also sure.

I saw the Holy City, the new Jerusalem, coming down out of heaven from God, prepared as a bride beautifully dressed for her husband. And I heard a loud voice from the throne saying, "Now the dwelling of God is with men, and he will live with them. They will be his people, and God himself will be with them and be their God. He will wipe every tear from their eyes. There will be no more death or mourning or crying or pain, for the old order of things has passed away." He who was seated on the throne said, "I am making everything new!" Then he said, "Write this down, for these words are trustworthy and true." He said to me: "It is done. I am the Alpha and the Omega, the Beginning and the End."[79]

---

[78] Revelation 19:11 – 16, 20; 20:10.
[79] Revelation 21:2 – 6.

11

A MISSIONARY'S STORY

The devil is aware that one hour of intimate, spiritual and earnest communion with God in prayer, is able to pull down what he has been contriving and building many a year.

John Flavel

In early 1992 my wife, Becky, and I had been in East Africa for a little over a year. We had been sent there as missionaries with the goal of bringing the gospel to the Sandawe people, an unreached people group in central Tanzania. Our son, who I'll call Junior, was 3 ½ years old, and our first daughter was not yet a year old. We had just learned that Becky was pregnant with our second daughter. Her morning sickness, combined with the heat and the still-new culture that surrounded us, was raising our stress levels to new heights. We were living in a small city while I took trips to a little village in the bush that was situated in the Sandawe area. I was building a simple house there. My Tanzanian co-worker, Hubiri, was already in that village working with the Sandawe people. We earnestly wanted to be with him and his family so that our missionary team could be on-site and complete.

It was at this time that we experienced an attack on our son that taught us much about spiritual conflict with the devil. I pass this experience on to you with the prayer that you will learn from it too.

He began to awaken at night with out-of-control crying. He would become frantic. His eyes would often be open but he showed no signs that he could see us or anything else in the room. Terror was etched on his face and filled his cries. We feared for him and were overwhelmed with helplessness as we struggled to physically restrain him and calm him down. We would talk with him, hold him, pray with him, but nothing seemed to help. Sometimes it would take a half an hour before he would calm down and go back to sleep.

I will let my journal entries of those days tell the story.

> April 28. I must record a bit about Junior. There has been a decided turn for the worse with him—a great showing of insecurity. He is crying at the drop of a hat. And the occasions of awaking at night and crying have increased. To be honest—I am very apprehensive about leaving Becky with the kids on this trip to the village. Even last night Junior awoke and cried for close to 20 minutes or more before settling down. We are at a loss to explain this. We fall at the Lord's feet for help.

> April 30. While gone on this trip Junior did well. We've shared our burden with others, and they are praying with us.

> May 3. Junior woke up from his nap with the same crying routine yesterday. It puts me at a complete loss to know what to do.

Even though I was praying against Satan's involvement in these crying episodes, I was still trying to figure out if it was only demonic or if there were other causes as well.

> May 7. Last night Junior woke up crying again. This time he had fallen out of bed and was tangled up in the mosquito net. At first I thought he was crying because of the fall. But as it went on, I realized that it was the same thing that has been happening. It is so frustrating for me. We must get help. Is it demons? Is it something physical? A combination of the two? Or emotional? O Lord—show us the answer I pray.

> May 12. Must record something very interesting from the last trip to the village. At one point I was sharing in detail with Hubiri the concern we have for Junior and his awakening at night crying. Kurt [a missionary from the same city where we lived who had gone with me on that trip] was there, and he shared that his son has the same problem. Many of the symptoms are exactly the same. Then he shared that he knows of two other missionary families in the same city who are having the same thing happen with their children.

> The conversation with Kurt and Hubiri makes me think that this is demonic activity. It appears that Satan is busy attacking the children of missionaries in an attempt to spoil the work. May God lead us, and give us wisdom and courage.

As time went on, I became more and more convinced that the root cause of our son's problem was indeed a demonic attack.

May 20. This afternoon Junior awoke from his nap crying again—not as severe as some times in the past...he was more "with it" and able to interact with me...but was very agitated and crying. At one point I asked if he had had a bad dream. He nodded "yes," but when asked to explain said that he didn't want to. About 20 minutes later we were all in the car (he was back to his normal self) and the subject of his dream came up. At that point he shared that the devil had been there threatening to hurt him. Junior said that he quoted John 3:16 to the devil, and the devil left—but that he was still afraid.

I need to back up now and record, as best as I can remember, another conversation I had with Junior. The exact date I don't remember. I was putting Junior to bed for the night, and he was particularly anxious and clingy. He didn't want me to leave. I was beginning to get frustrated—but decided to approach it differently and get him talking. Our conversation went like this:

"Junior, are you afraid of something?"

"Yes."

"Are you afraid of bad dreams?"

"Yeah."

"Well, I've had bad dreams too. I just resist the devil in Jesus' name and have the bad dream go away."

"What does the devil look like?"

"Oh, I don't know exactly. He can change himself to look like even a good angel. The Bible says that. So he can look many different ways."

"Is the devil a liar?"

"Yes."

"What lies does he tell?"

"Oh, many. Too many to say."

"Can he kill you?"

"Junior, has the devil told you that he is going to kill you?"

Junior nodded yes.

"Junior, did you know that God says in the Bible that He will protect you from the devil." Then I quoted 1 John 5:18 to him: "We know that everyone who has been born of God does not keep on sinning, but he who was born of God [i.e. Jesus] protects him, and the evil one does not touch him."

And so we discussed some basic principles of resisting the devil with Scripture like Jesus did. That conversation of a few weeks ago, and this one today, sure shows evidence of demonic activity. I'm still not ready to count out any physical or emotional factors. There is a lot of stress in our household, in our lives, at the moment. No doubt this stress is felt by Junior and could exhibit itself in various ways.

Nevertheless, we must confront the evidence of demonic activity. God will bring complete victory.

May 26. Last night Junior began what looked like would be another session of crying. I immediately knelt by his bed and began definite warfare praying against the evil forces who have been assigned to Junior. Junior settled into a peaceful sleep…he never woke up at all. We will continue using the weapons of the Spirit until there is complete victory.

June 6. Interesting. Last night I was up but everyone else had gone to bed. I heard Junior begin to cry and fret so I immediately went in, knelt by his bed, held his hand, and began praying. Praying again in a more definite and pointed way—resisting the evil one and binding any plans of evil that have been formed against Junior. Junior settled and slept peacefully.

This morning at breakfast I asked him if he had any dreams last night. He said, "no," but then he said that Satan had tried to come to him last night, but the Lord had protected him and Satan left.

"I didn't even have to quote verses to Satan this time—he just left. Satan came to try to give me a bad dream, but the Lord held me."

Thank you, Lord, for your hand of protection, for picking up my little boy and holding him in your arms.

We saw temporary victories but not a final deliverance. I sensed God's leading to begin a fast.

*Fast &
pray*

June 7. Still trouble with Junior. It has been three times in a row now. Yesterday's nap. Last night. Today's nap. I've decided on another season of prayer and fasting. Three items to concentrate on. (1) Deliverance for Junior from these attacks. (2) For the Sandawe: I hope to participate in the work there this week through prayer rather than a visit. (3) Becky. Her health, and other needs.

Lord, do lead, I pray. Direct. Give insight. Give power. Give deliverance to our son. Give Yourself glory in the Sandawe.

June 8. Am starting a season of prayer. Hope to fast for three days.

June 9. Good prayer time last night. Then this morning and around noon the Lord graciously gave some more good times with Him. The headaches of yesterday are gone. Good focused time in prayer. The Lord has chastened me…God has first pressed home some lessons for my own life. I am beginning to sense the freedom to move outward now in my prayers.

June 10. Good times in prayer this morning, this afternoon, and now this evening. Have sensed power and freedom in interceding for Hubiri and the Sandawe. Have begun to formulate a plan of action concerning Junior's attacks. God is giving light.

Also, since I began this fast, Becky has had no nausea. The Lord is answering my prayers concerning her health. Also, her spirit. I've been praying that God would replace the spirit of fainting with a mantle of praise. I can see evidence of that also.

May God continue giving insight, direction, and focus in prayer. Although this time of fasting has been somewhat more difficult on me than previous times, there has been tremendous blessing. Personal renewal. Insight from the Lord concerning specific issues. Answers to specific prayer. Freedom and focus in prayer. I thank God for His gracious help to me.

June 11. Another good session of prayer this morning before breaking the fast. When I awoke my heart was pounding, and I felt bad. I made my way to the bathroom where I broke into a sweat and was on the verge of vomiting. This lasted for a while. I tried to relax and pray. After a while the nausea subsided enough for me to get to the kitchen and drink some water. As I drank and began my prayer time, the nausea vanished and I was able to enter into a fruitful time.

I remember a point during that morning's prayer time that I had the distinct sense that something happened. I was praying earnestly for Junior's deliverance, and although I did not see or hear anything, I had the strong impression that something broke. At that moment, I knew that God was going to deliver Junior. The battle was over—even though I had not yet gotten up off my knees.

[Continuing on June 11] It has been truly encouraging. God will grant deliverance. Be it quick or lingering—the problem will be overcome.

I have also enjoyed intercession for Hubiri and his family, and for the Sandawe people. And of most importance—good times of intercession on behalf of my wife.

God is so good. Truly I am weak, but in His grace he continues to minister to me. Thank You, Lord.

Future entries in my journal documented how marvelously God answered prayer.

June 13. Had a missionary family over for supper last night. That was a good time. The first time Becky has felt up to having people over in a long time. Thank You, Lord, for lifting the morning sickness.

June 14. Today I received a letter by bus from Hubiri. What an encouragement! It appears that three people gave their lives to Christ on the 11th. That was the day after my last full day of the fast, which was the day I prayed for the Sandawe more so than the other days. God is so good!

June 24. Since the last day of my season in prayer—since moving forward in the plan that the Lord gave me regarding Junior's night-time problem—there has been no reoccurrence of the bad dreams. Praise to the Almighty! We continue to pray aggressively and not let up…but it appears that this enemy has retreated. Hallelujah!

It was true—the nighttime visitations from the evil one to the little 3 ½ year-old ceased instantaneously. The nightmares were over. The attack had been broken. Jesus Christ—the one who died on the cross, the one who rose from the dead and ascended into heaven, the one who comes to little children in their fear and holds them, the one who answers the prayers of desperate parents—delivered our boy from the devil. May our Lord Jesus receive all our praise!

12

DREAMS

In peace I will both lie down and sleep; for you alone, O Lord, make me dwell in safety.
King David

I don't fully understand what happens with our mind and spirit when we are dreaming. I have read scientific explanations about the dream state of our minds and watched documentaries about the brain and dreams. It seems obvious to me that the ones writing the papers and making the documentaries don't have all their questions answered, either.

What I do know is that it is not unusual for demonic attacks to occur when we are asleep, and that we experience these attacks in dreams. One of the most common questions I am asked when people are given the freedom to talk about their experiences with the unseen realm is, "Does Satan have influence on, or involvement in, my dreams?" The quick answer is, "yes." But let's think about this issue further.

The human being is amazingly complex. With every advance in our understanding of human biology and psychology, we see deeper meaning in David's prayer, "I praise you, for I am fearfully and wonderfully made."[80] I have already explained in chapter 9 that the devil is not our only source of trouble, for we also deal with the flesh and the world. Discernment is needed at times to realize exactly where our problem is coming from and how we are to respond. In the same way, within each person there is more than one factor contributing to his or her experience. Physical, mental, emotional, and spiritual factors all play a part in what we perceive and how we respond, and all of these factors are involved when we are asleep as well as when we are awake.

We should not automatically attribute a bad dream to the presence of an evil one. It might be caused by medicine we are taking or by some imbalance in our body's chemistry. It could also occur because we've focused our thoughts all day long on some negative issue, or we watched alarming things on the television or internet, or we recently have been living in an unhealthy emotional state. Many factors can contribute to a bad dream.

Having said that, however, there is no doubt in my mind that at times when we are sleeping, Satan either piggybacks on one or more of these other factors, or he attacks for no fault of our own, and we experience the attack in a dream. Fear is almost always involved. Sometimes there is the presentation of evil in the form of obvious sins. At other times there is deception involved—the dream leaves you thinking about things that you normally would not allow yourself to dwell on. Finally, in some cases, you actually see an evil being.

There can be a connection between anxiety and nighttime attacks. Before I became a Christian, I was a very anxious person. Worry had become a pattern in my life. Since my conversion, God has greatly changed me, but I am always aware of the underlying tendency to worry—a tendency that my early years ingrained on my personality. I tell you this because I want you to know that I

---

80   Psalm 139:14.

have learned the hard way about the connection between worry and attacks in dreams.

The New Testament instructs us as follows:

> Do not be anxious about anything, but in everything by prayer and supplication with thanksgiving let your requests be made known to God. And the peace of God, which surpasses all understanding, will guard your hearts and your minds in Christ Jesus.[81]

Notice, first of all, that we are commanded not to worry. "Do not be anxious about anything." Second, notice that the peace of God comes through prayer. By bringing the issues over which we are worrying to the Lord in prayer, we gain his peace. This is not always an instantaneous experience, but if we persevere, it is a sure and real experience. Third, notice that this peace that we have gained protects us. "And the peace of God…will guard your hearts and your minds."

Guard our hearts and minds *from what*? The verse does not explicitly tell us what we are being guarded against. I suggest that we are being guarded against whatever it is we need to be protected from, and that certainly includes Satan!

When I lie down to sleep at night and am worrying, I am forfeiting a portion of God's protection.

I do not pretend to understand the complexity of how this works in terms of my own psychology, its intersection with the spiritual realm, and God's gracious dealings with us. But I do understand that this principle is true. If I go to sleep in an anxious state, I open a door for the devil. If I pray over what I'm worrying about until I have his peace, and then go to bed, I sleep with that door shut against the devil.

---

[81]   Philippians 4:6 – 7.

Don't go to sleep with anxiety.

Worry is not the only way we set ourselves up for trouble in our dreams. Our spiritual battle with the devil is not a separate issue from our experience of controlling our fleshly desires. A man or woman who spends much of their day dwelling on sensuality will find their daytime thought-life reflected in their dreams. Sometimes Satan capitalizes on our daytime fixations and works it for evil while we sleep. This possibility is as real for issues like covetousness, violence, and bitterness as it is for sensuality.

When you are attacked in your dreams, whether through some fault of your own or not, you will often wake up. At that point you need to look to the Lord in prayer, claim the blood of Christ for any fault that may have been yours, and then resist the devil. If you are married, and the attack was particularly strong, wake your spouse and pray together. Resist the devil, and he will flee from you.

Here is a way of praying and resisting when awakened with a dream that Satan was using.

Father, I ask for your help. Forgive me for any way in which I contributed to this dream. I claim afresh the blood of Christ that cleanses us from all sin. Now, Satan, I rebuke you away from me in Jesus' name because the Word of God says, "Resist the devil, and he will flee from you." You must flee now!

After you become used to putting into practice that which I am teaching you in this book, you may find yourself resisting the devil while still in a dream state. This is more common than you might expect. In the cases when an evil being is seen, and you do not immediately wake up, you can resist the devil in your dream and have him flee. This has happened to me and to others I know.

Even though the devil can attack at night, we do not have to be afraid. As *Elizabeth's Story* shows (chapter 7), there is no need for nighttime attacks to be the norm. Satan can be pushed back, and attacks in our dreams can become very infrequent, almost non-existent. Those that do come, we handle as we always do, and bow to God's sovereignty in allowing them.

My wife and I pray for God's protection over us before we go to sleep. It is a bedtime practice that we rarely miss. When our children were in the home, our prayers always included them. Even though they are now adults living in faraway places, we still often find ourselves including them in our nightly prayers for protection.

I give you here a sample of how we pray at night. It isn't always the same, and there is no magic in the particular words, but the idea is represented below. As I lay in bed, I mentally start at the border of our property and then pray inward until I'm talking to God about our dreams.

O Lord, we ask in Jesus' name that you would give your angels a charge concerning us[82] and our property as we sleep. Please keep the evil one away from all our property, our house, and this room. Protect us in our sleep. Keep the evil one away from our dreams, Lord, and give us good dreams. Thank you for your protection. Amen.

The conflict in the spiritual realm does not end just because we go to sleep, but neither does God's protection.

"If you lie down, you will not be afraid; when you lie down, your sleep will be sweet."[83]

---

[82]   This kind of language is taken from Psalm 91. I discuss this in chapter 22.
[83]   Proverbs 3:24.

13

WHEN THE CONFLICT IS PROTRACTED

Adversity is the diamond dust Heaven polishes its jewels with.

Robert Leighton

Usually there is immediate relief after resisting the devil. We resist and he flees. But sometimes it is not so straightforward. There can be strong intransigence and a protracted conflict.

I will suggest three possible reasons for protracted spiritual struggle, but as you consider my thoughts keep in mind there is a certain element of mystery that is associated with the unseen realm. We must be content with not knowing all the answers while we continue in the spiritual fight.

First, there is a sanctifying purpose in the mind of God for allowing the delay.

No matter what kind of trial we experience in life, we know that God is using the difficulty to produce the personal growth that he desires for us.

> Count it all joy, my brothers, when you meet trials of
> various kinds, for you know that the testing of your
> faith produces steadfastness. And let steadfastness
> have its full effect, that you may be perfect and
> complete, lacking in nothing.[84]

Notice in the above verses that we meet "various kinds" of trials. One kind of trial is that of being under spiritual attack in which the enemy persists even though we are resisting. The purpose of God in that trial is no different than in any other kind of trial—God is using it to mold us into the kind of people that he wants us to be. God knows how long we need to be under a particular difficulty in order for him to accomplish the life-change he desires in us.

Our part is submission. We bow to God's sovereignty and accept what he is allowing, even as we continue in the spiritual battle.

Second, there is something in our life that needs to be removed.

This "something" may be a moral issue, or in some cases a physical object. Whatever the case, there is a cleansing that needs to take place, and our victory is contingent upon the cleansing.

It is interesting to me that after Jesus' temptation in the wilderness in which his last words to Satan were "be gone!" his first word to people was "repent!"[85] In some places in Scripture, the demons are referred to as "unclean spirits."[86] If we are unclean ourselves, yet trying to dislodge one of them, we are likely to fail. As we are wrestling with a resistant spirit, we must search our own hearts and make the psalmist's prayer our own, "Search me, O God, and know my heart! Try me and know my thoughts! And see if there be any grievous way in me, and lead me in the way everlasting!"[87]

---

[84] James 1:2 – 4.

[85] Matthew 4:17.

[86] Matthew 12:43; Mark 1:23, 26; 3:30; 5:2, 8; 7:25; 9:25; Luke 8:29; 9:42;
11:24; Revelation 18:2.

[87] Psalm 139:23 – 24.

God always answers that prayer. Once we confess and forsake our sin, we will find new strength in the battle.

You will remember that in *A Missionary's Story* (chapter 11) I entered into the season of prayer with three issues on my mind: my wife, my son, and our missionary work. As I sought God, however, he directed my attention first to my own failings. It was only after responding with confession and repentance that I could move forward into prayer for spiritual deliverance.

There is also the very real issue of physical objects that have demonic influence attached to them.

> And a number of those who had practiced magic arts brought their books together and burned them in the sight of all. And they counted the value of them and found it came to fifty thousand pieces of silver. So the word of the Lord continued to increase and prevail mightily.[88]

Even though Luke, the author of Acts, does not say that there were evil spirits attached to the books, we recognize that the books had been used in demonic activity. That example encourages us to show our repentance by renouncing anything we own that has some obvious link with the unseen realm.

Some objects that find their way into our homes have been used by others in occult practices. It is also possible that we ourselves had a personal history in the occult, or in other dangerous spiritual practices, and although we have stopped doing those things, the paraphernalia we used is still in our home. In some cases Christian travelers have naively bought what they thought were innocent carvings or "local art" and by doing so introduced into their houses things associated with evil spirits. How, exactly, physical objects

---

[88]　Acts 19:19 – 20.

become associated with an evil spirit, I do not know. But I do know that it occurs and that action must be taken to eliminate the satanic influence. We follow the example of the above verses and dispose of the objects.

I see an appalling naivety on the part of American Christians in this regard. Artwork, books, DVDs, posters, videos, computer games, and other objects that refer directly to witchcraft or other demonic activity are kept in the home. In the case of the games, these objects are not only present but invite regular participation. It is possible that one or more of those objects has a spirit associated with it. Why take that chance? We are told to "be on the alert"[89] for our enemy. Having the devil's things in our house doesn't sound to me like we are being alert.

Cleanse your home. It is a helpful exercise for you and your family members to prayerfully take a walk through your home, and ask God to show you what needs to be thrown out. Also, it is no accident that Acts 19:19 – 20 makes a point of telling us how much the books cost. Fifty thousand pieces of silver was an enormous value in that day.[90] You may hesitate to dispose of something because of what you paid for it. If so, you now face a decision. What is worth more to you: the object or your freedom from Satan?

Before leaving this subject, I want to add that sometimes an ordinary object that has no obvious outward association with evil can, in fact, become of some importance or use to evil spirits. Again, we don't understand why or how, but *Terrance's Story* illustrates that this can indeed happen.

---

[89] 1 Peter 5:8.

[90] There were two coins of silver in the days of Acts, the denarii and the drachma. If the "pieces of silver" referred to denarii, it would have been the equivalent of 137 years of wages. If they were drachma, it would have been the equivalent of enough bread for 100 families for 500 days. Either way, it was an extremely large monetary value.

Terrance's Story

My wife and I had been married only about five years. We didn't have a lot of money, and even though we were able to buy a simple little home, we didn't have money for furniture. A lady we knew from our church somehow heard we were looking for furniture and gave us a little chest of drawers. I stripped the paint from it, repainted it, and put it in the extra bedroom.

From time to time when I was in that room I would begin to feel uneasy. I had learned a little bit about spiritual warfare, so I wasn't totally ignorant about those kinds of things. Anyway, I prayed in that room—and my wife and I prayed together in the room—against any evil spirits that may have been there.

Time went on and I would still feel uneasy in the room. At one point, as I was in there praying and asking the Lord for wisdom, my attention went to the chest of drawers. I walked over to it and felt led to pray over it. I had never done anything like that before. It might sound crazy, but that is what I did. I don't know how to explain it except that God was leading me. So, I prayed against any evil spirit that might have been assigned to the chest of drawers.

I did that several times because I would often feel odd when I entered that room, like something was wrong. Well, my brother, who is sensitive to this kind of thing, came for an overnight visit. We put him in the extra room. I didn't say anything to him, just prayed. In the morning he said, "Terrance, there is definitely something wrong in that room!"

Well, finally, even though we had prayed a lot over the chest of drawers, we decided to get rid of it. So, with one final rebuking of the devil, we got that piece of furniture out of our home. All the uneasiness and weird feelings left. There was never another bad experience in the room for ourselves or anyone else.

And get this—we later learned that the woman who gave it to us had been deep into the occult before she became a Christian!

Third, there is a conflict in the spiritual realm that we cannot see.

There is a fascinating story in the book of Daniel that hints at another reason why victory in a spiritual conflict can take longer than expected. Daniel had been praying earnestly for three weeks, at which time he saw a heavenly being in a vision.

And behold, a hand touched me and set me trembling on my hands and knees. And he said to me, "O Daniel, man greatly loved, understand the words that I speak to you, and stand upright, for now I have been sent to you." And when he had spoken this word to me, I stood up trembling. Then he said to me, "Fear not, Daniel, for from the first day that you set your heart to understand and humbled yourself before your God, your words have been heard, and I have come because of your words. The prince of the kingdom of Persia withstood me twenty-one days, but Michael, one of the chief princes, came to help me, for I was left there with the kings of Persia, and came to make you understand what is to happen to your people in the latter days. For the vision is for days yet to come."[91]

The angel had been dispatched to go to Daniel immediately when Daniel began his praying. But the "prince of the kingdom of Persia" got in the way of this angel. This "prince" was some sort of powerful evil spirit. The angel and evil spirit clashed until Michael the archangel[92] came and helped. At that time the angel made his way to Daniel. The answer to Daniel's prayer was delayed because of an unseen conflict. Truly there are aspects of our wrestling with the devil that would amaze us if they could be seen!

Daniel couldn't see that angelic conflict, but he could see the delay. What did he do in that delay? He kept praying. That is what we do when there is a delay of deliverance—we keep on seeking God's face and resisting the devil.

In addition to submitting to God's will, examining and cleansing your life, and persisting in the battle knowing that you cannot see all that is going on, there are two other pieces of advice that I have for you.

Fast and pray, and believe.

There is a telling episode in Jesus' ministry where a father came to Jesus for help for his boy who had an evil spirit.[93] Jesus was not

---

91   Daniel 10:10 – 14.

92   Michael is called the Archangel in Jude 9 and in Revelation 12:7.

93   You may want to read the entire episode. It is in Matthew 17:14 – 20 and Mark 9:14 – 29.

there at that time, and so the disciples tried to cast it out themselves. These same disciples had succeeded in situations like this before, but this time they failed. Jesus arrived, took stock of the situation, and cast out the evil spirit. The perplexed disciples asked Jesus why they failed. Both Matthew and Mark record this occurrence, and each chose to record a different part of the conversation that ensued.

> Mark wrote, "And he said to them, 'This kind cannot be driven out by anything but prayer.'"[94]

> Matthew wrote, "He said to them, 'Because of your little faith.'"[95]

"This kind" of evil spirit put up a bigger fight than the disciples were used to. Their faith wavered. Apparently, they were not living in the state of prayer that is necessary to bolster faith during this kind of conflict. And so they failed. Jesus was living in prayer—full of faith—and won the conflict.

Some Greek manuscripts of the New Testament add the word "and fasting" to Mark 9:29, and so certain English versions read, "This kind cannot be driven out by anything but prayer and fasting."[96] The uncertainty about whether or not the reference to fasting was in Mark's original writing does not bother me because the purpose of fasting is to intensify prayer. When I fast, I find more clarity and power in my praying, and therefore I experience more expansive faith.

There are times when a prolonged trial calls for fasting. Our prayer is intensified. In such prayer we find ourselves with greater faith, claiming our position in Christ and resisting the evil one with Spirit-led confidence. I would encourage you to be open to the Lord's leading, and add fasting to your praying when there is a prolonged demonic trial.

---

94   Mark 9:29.
95   Matthew 17:20.
96   New King James and Young's Literal Translation.

Lift up the exalted Christ in presence of the evil one.

Christ is exalted far above the enemy we are facing. The reason we can resist is that we are in Christ. The evil one who is giving us trouble is inferior to Christ, is defeated by Christ's death and resurrection, and has no authority over us. It is helpful to rehearse these truths out loud to the evil presence when there is prolonged resistance. When we do so, we quote Scriptures that declare Satan's subservience to the Lord Jesus.[97] By doing this we bolster our own faith and, at the same time, weaken the enemy.

The certainty of our authority in Christ, and the absolute victory he has accomplished, does not mean that the outworking of his victory in our lives comes without a struggle. After all, it was not easy for Jesus, and in his difficulty, he showed us the value of endurance.

> Therefore, since we are surrounded by so great a cloud of witnesses, let us also lay aside every weight, and sin which clings so closely, and let us run with endurance the race that is set before us, looking to Jesus, the founder and perfecter of our faith, who for the joy that was set before him endured the cross, despising the shame, and is seated at the right hand of the throne of God.[98]

We will follow his example, endure through prolonged trials, and share in his victory.

---

[97] Ephesians 1:20 – 23 and Philippians 2:9 – 11 can be used in this kind of situation.

[98] Hebrews 12:1 – 2.

14

PROTECTING OUR CHILDREN

If you neglect to instruct your children in the way of holiness, will the devil neglect to instruct them in the way of wickedness? No. If ground be uncultivated, weeds will spring.

John Flavel

Perhaps you have seen a movie in which there is a sword fight between a hero and a villain. The bad guy drops his sword and the gentleman stops, allows the antagonist to reclaim his weapon, and then resumes the fight. Unfortunately, Satan does not fight like a gentleman. Nothing makes this fact more evident than his attacks on our children.

Satan's intent is to steal, kill, and destroy. Satan's nature is to lie. He ruthlessly pursues all this evil with children as well as with adults. We are aware of Scripture's injunction to "be on the alert."[99] Parents need to be alert, not only for themselves, but for

---

[99]   1 Peter 5:8.

their children, especially when our children are small and less able to watch for themselves. As children grow older, their parents need to teach them about resisting, so that the children themselves are equipped for the battle.

Recently I was at an outdoor gathering of friends and family. It was a beautiful fall day, and one of my daughters walked up to my left side and put her arm in mine. We began walking down a path side by side, arm in arm. At the end of the pathway was a young man facing us with a broad smile. It was my daughter's wedding. If there was any doubt before, it was all gone on that day—my "little girl" was no longer a child. The memory of her wedding sits juxtaposed in my mind with my memories of the day she was born. At one point a midwife handed her to me, and I held her, tiny and helpless, in the crook of my left arm—the same arm she held on to as I escorted her to her groom. Between those two experiences there was a transition from childhood to adulthood. In that transition my responsibilities also went through a transformation. I had to make adjustments along the way. As her capacity to think and make decisions increased, I had to give her more information and freedom. As she matured, I had to gradually treat her less as a child and more as an adult. In the early years, my wife and I did more for her, and used our authority to ensure that she was involved in certain practices. Later we would encourage her but could not force her to engage in those same practices.

Several times in this book, I've mentioned the means of grace. The practices of reading the Bible, praying, living in community with other believers, serving, being baptized, and taking communion, all with the heart attitudes of faith and obedience, are much more than "churchy things" that someone somewhere decided that Christians are supposed to do. They are the divinely-ordained means by which God pours grace into our lives. When we avail ourselves of those means, God enlivens us spiritually. When we avoid or neglect them, we begin to shrivel up.

And so it is with our children.

We remember that there are three sources of spiritual trouble: the world, the flesh, and the devil. These three sources create trouble for us whether we are children or adults. The use of the means of grace is our primary way of experiencing God's life and joy and power in the face of those trouble sources. When our children are young, we must work hard to instill habits in them concerning the means of grace. Our efforts, however, need to be matched with our example. They must see us participating in the means of grace and experiencing the life of God while they receive instruction from us on how to use them for themselves. Our everyday experience of the grace of God, coupled with their expanding personal experience in the means of grace, is one of the greatest ways we can protect our children.

Another vital component in children's protection is their parent's prayers for them. There is mystery in prayer, and theologians argue over how prayer fits within God's sovereignty, but this I know—Jesus invites us to pray and promises that God will answer.[100] When parents intercede for their children it has a powerful effect on the family. Pray daily for your children—you will never count that time wasted.

At this point, I would like to have a word with passive dads. It pains me to see so many mothers actively instilling the means of grace into their children while the father hovers nearby, watching but not participating. It is even more alarming to see the father lost in the background when there is evidence of demonic attack while the mother leads the way in resisting Satan. From one dad to another, let me say this—get off your duff and own up to your spiritual authority in the home! Your children's spiritual welfare is at stake.

---

100   Matthew 7:7 – 11. "Ask, and it will be given to you; seek, and you will find; knock, and it will be opened to you. For everyone who asks receives, and the one who seeks finds, and to the one who knocks it will be opened. Or which one of you, if his son asks him for bread, will give him a stone? Or if he asks for a fish, will give him a serpent? If you then, who are evil, know how to give good gifts to your children, how much more will your Father who is in heaven give good things to those who ask him!"

We are told in Scripture, "For the husband is the head of the wife even as Christ is the head of the church."[101] There is a vast and energetic discussion going on in American Christianity about the meaning of the husband's headship. It is a very important issue and involves some passages of Scripture that are challenging to interpret, and so it is good that we are having the conversation. I am afraid, however, that a simple truth can be lost in the heat and smoke of our deliberations: for the husband to reflect in his home the headship of Christ in the church, something will be different about how he relates to his wife as compared to how his wife relates to him. She is not the head; he is.

I believe that, as the head of the home, the father has a responsibility and corresponding authority that differs somewhat from that of the mother. When the father is not taking initiative in training the children or praying for them, there is a spiritual shortfall in the home. In the same way, when there is a spiritual attack and the father lets the wife lead the way, he has missed an opportunity to add strength to the protection of his home. Fathers, own up to your spiritual authority, and lead the way in protecting your family!

And wives, I have just a short word of advice to you. If your husband has been deficient in this regard, and in response to God's working in his heart decides to step up and take initiative where he has historically failed, please let him lead. He may not do everything the way you would have or could have, but now you have a husband who is shouldering his responsibility and authority in your home. Encourage any steps he takes in this direction, and watch what God will do!

In some homes the mother has been left to herself to provide all the spiritual input and protection for the children. For whatever reason, the father is not in the picture. If that is your situation, please do not be dismayed. First, you are the mother. To say that there is a unique authority in the headship of the father is not to say

---

[101]   Ephesians 5:23.

that there is no authority in you. On the contrary, you can stand tall in the name of Christ, and in your role of mother, and see the strength of the Lord in your children's lives. Second, the Lord has a special concern for widows and orphans.[102] I believe this concern is expressed to women who are not actually widows, but have been left to themselves in the spiritual training of their children. You can count on God's help. Third, God uses the believing spouse as a sanctifying influence on the children.[103] Even though on some days you cannot see it clearly, God is indeed using you. Fourth, the body of believers in which you participate, your church, can be the source of Christian men who provide the role models that your children need. And finally, the leaders in the church can apply their authority to their prayers for your children. God will "fill in the gaps" and help you be everything you need to be for your children.

Our children can be targeted by the evil one through no fault of theirs or their parents. That is the nature of our existence on earth. When an attack comes, we can take all that we have learned about resisting the devil and apply it on behalf of our children.

Linda's Story

This happened more than once for me and my husband when the kids were small—younger than ten years old. They would be playing in the house, and soon there would be bickering. Then it would get worse, and there would be big spats over little things. Either my husband or I would correct them, as we normally would,

---

102   Psalm 68:5; James 1:27.
103   1 Corinthians 7:14.

but the fighting would continue. We would correct them again, and still the kids would be agitated and on edge. Of course, our kids had spats at other times, but they usually responded to our discipline. This seemed different. There was nothing we knew of that was upsetting them. We hadn't filled them up with red Kool Aid or sugar! What was the problem?

Finally, I went to my husband and said, "This is not normal. We need to resist the devil." He agreed, so we went into another room and shut the door. We could still hear the kids bickering out in the living room. My husband started praying. We confessed our sin, claimed the blood of Christ, and then we rebuked the devil.

We said something like, *Satan, in the name of Jesus Christ, we rebuke you. This is our home, and we have dedicated it to the glory of Jesus Christ. These are our children, and we claim them for Jesus Christ. You have no right here, and we demand that you go. Now! For the Word of God says, "Greater is he who is in us than he who is in the world!"*[104]

It was my husband who did the rebuking, and when he was finished I said a firm, *"Amen!"* It was like someone threw a light switch! Immediately everything changed. The kids didn't know where we were or what we were doing, but when we came back to the living

---

[104] 1 John 4:4.

> room, there they were playing quietly—no
> more fighting. All the spirit of agitation was
> gone from the home. Praise the Lord!

When Jesus' disciples asked him to teach them to pray, he gave them a model prayer to follow that we know as The Lord's Prayer. In that pattern, we find these words:

> And lead us not into temptation, but deliver us
> from evil.[105]

On the night that Jesus was betrayed, he prayed for his disciples. In that prayer, we find these words:

> Holy Father, keep them in your name, which you
> have given me...While I was with them, I kept them
> in your name, which you have given me. I have
> guarded them, and not one of them has been lost
> except the son of destruction, that the Scripture
> might be fulfilled.... I do not ask that you take
> them out of the world, but that you keep them from
> the evil one. [106]

In both prayers we see Jesus being aware of the presence of evil and asking God for protection. We have his example and all the promises of God behind us as we get on our knees to ask God to protect our children. It would be hard to over-emphasize the importance of prayer in this regard.

In Ephesians 6, the Apostle Paul uses the example of a Roman soldier's armor to illustrate how we can be equipped for our spiritual

---

[105] Matthew 6:13.
[106] John 17:11 – 12, 15.

battle. Six pieces of armor are mentioned with their corresponding meaning: the belt, the breastplate, the boots, the shield, the helmet, and the sword. It would be a mistake, however, to conclude that only six points were being made by Paul. There is a seventh. After naming the six, he begins explaining the seventh, and it appears that he becomes so intent on explaining its vital part in our spiritual battle that he leaves the illustration of armor behind. He is no longer concerned with the illustration—he wants to emphasize this one remaining item. That item is prayer.

> Praying at all times in the Spirit, with all prayer and supplication. To that end keep alert with all perseverance, making supplication for all the saints.[107]

Notice that the word "all" occurs four times in that verse. He wants Spirit-enabled prayer to be made at *all* times, and that *all* kinds of prayer be made, and that we do so with *all* perseverance, and that we pray for *all* Christians. It has been suggested that prayer is vital to using all of the other six pieces of armor. I agree, and yet, it is also a weapon in its own right.

We can learn to pray aggressively against the work of the evil one and to do so on behalf of other people, especially our own children.

My wife and I have a favorite picture, which we've hung in our various homes over the last few decades. It is the work of an artist named Ron DiCianni, which he titled *Spiritual Warfare*. When we saw it, we immediately bought a copy, framed it, and put it in our home. When you first look at it your eye is drawn to a father who is kneeling in prayer at the bedside of his sleeping child. If your attention lingers there you notice that the time on the father's watch is near midnight. Eventually your eye moves to the open window, past the curtains blowing in the night breeze, and to the sky outside.

---

107 Ephesians 6:18.

What you first thought was the play of moonlight on the clouds reveals itself to be a battle going on between an evil one and an angel. The good angel is positioned with its back towards the scene inside, defending the home. If you continue to let the picture guide your eyes, the moonlight will pull your attention back inside. There you'll see what you had initially missed, that the moonlight shining through the window panes casts a shadow in the shape of a cross that falls over the praying father and his sleeping child. Conflict in the unseen realm. Our children's need for protection. The cross. Prayer.

The unseen realm is exactly that: unseen. Nevertheless, we do know that as we engage in prayer, God answers, and there are results in that realm. Your children need your prayers.

There are times when someone is exerting a negative influence in the life of your child. It could be a classmate in school, or an extended family member, or a co-worker. It could be when your child is any age. As a parent you become concerned, and it may be that you are not in a position to prevent your child from coming into contact with that person. How do you pray in this case? First, you talk to the Lord in worship and confession. Then pray about the situation. And then momentarily change your focus to address the devil with words like these:

Satan, in the name of Jesus Christ, I rebuke you away from my daughter (or son). All your plans to use (name the person) for evil in her life, I tear down in the authority of the Lord. For the Word of God says, "For the weapons of our warfare are not of the flesh but have divine power to destroy strongholds."[108] In the name of Christ, I tear down any stronghold that you are building against my daughter through that person.

After addressing Satan, you then turn your focus back to the Lord and continue praying. Once again the "fog" of the unseen

---

[108] 2 Corinthians 10:4.

realm comes into play here. This is a case in which you are not sensing an evil presence right where you are but are concerned about an evil plan by Satan against your child. I find real strength and help in rebuking the devil in cases like this.

There are times when we are concerned with what thoughts or ideas our children are entertaining. Are they beginning to stray from the truth that we have been careful to teach them? In addition to keeping the truth in their lives (in whatever way is appropriate according to their age), we can be behind the scenes, praying against deception. While interceding for them, you can momentarily confront Satan with words like these:

Satan, in the name of Jesus Christ, I rebuke you away from my son (or daughter). All your plans to confuse him concerning the truth and to lead him away from faith in Christ, I tear down in the authority of the Lord. For the Word of God says, "For the weapons of our warfare are not of the flesh but have divine power to destroy strongholds."[109] In the name of Christ I tear down any stronghold that you are building against my son.

Psalm 91 has become one of my favorite Scripture passages to use while praying for my children. Many Christians over many centuries have cherished the promises of protection expressed in that psalm. It famously represents the dangers we face by referring to lions and snakes. "You will tread on the lion and the adder; the young lion and the serpent you will trample underfoot."[110] Most people understand those animals in the psalm as only representations of danger, but for our many years in Africa, they were the actual danger as well.

It was not unusual for us to hear lions roaring behind our house at night. One evening we had three of them on our kitchen porch. Snakes were a continual problem. We had forest cobras, water cobras, spitting cobras, green mambas, black mambas, boomslangs, puff adders and other kinds of deadly snakes right around our house,

---

[109] 2 Corinthians 10:4.
[110] Psalm 91:13.

a few times in our vehicle, and even a time or two inside our home. What were we as parents to do? Psalm 91 became very real to us!

That psalm refers to angels and their role in protecting the people of God.

> For he will give his angels a charge concerning you,
> to guard you in all your ways.[111]

I cannot count the times I borrowed that language from Psalm 91 and meshed it into my prayers. I would ask God to "give his angels a charge" concerning my children, to protect them. As a matter of fact, I prayed for their protection every morning. The stories of our encounters with lions and snakes would fill their own book, but to the Lord's praise, although we lived in the midst of these creatures, we were not struck down by them.

Isn't it true, though, that even you yourself live in the midst of "lions and snakes"? The spiritual dangers around your children are just as real as the animals we faced. And as *A Missionary's Story* (chapter 11) makes clear, we faced those spiritual dangers, too. The promise of Psalm 91 applies to all dangers, be they physical or spiritual.

Another biblical phrase that people often borrow for their prayers is found in the story of Job. Satan complained that God had put a "hedge" around Job that was protecting him.[112] I know parents that regularly pray for the Lord to "put a hedge around" their children. Taking phrases from the Scripture that refer to God's protection and using them in your prayers for your children is a powerful practice.

There are times when we feel the need for others to join us in prayer. Sometimes an attack motivates you to ask others to pray for you. At other times your general sense of inadequacy in the face of the enormous challenge of parenting moves you to ask for help. Recruit others to pray for you and your family. Get together with

---

111   Psalm 91:11 New American Standard Bible, Updated Edition.
112   Job 1:10 "Have you not put a hedge around him and his house and all that he has, on every side?"

them to pray. The example and teaching of Scripture is that there is power in joint prayer.

A Pastor's Story

I was in an elders' meeting one evening at the church. We were working through our agenda items when there was a knock at the door of our meeting room. This was unusual. The church people knew when our elder meetings were scheduled and always tried not to interfere. One of our members, Leon, was at the door, his face etched with concern.

"Pastor, our son is having one of those episodes. I know that the elders are meeting tonight. I apologize for interrupting, but I wondered if you men could pray for him. Nothing we do seems to help. He's here, outside in the van with my wife."

I had met several times with Leon about his son. The boy was about 10 years old and suffered from bouts of extreme anxiety. We had prayed together, tried to think of all the possible ways to address the situation, and had begun resisting the devil.

I was so proud of how the elders rose to the occasion. They didn't hesitate but stopped the meeting and went out into the church parking lot. When we opened the van door and I leaned in, I saw weariness and fear on every face: the boy, his younger brother, his mother, and of course, the father. A combination of compassion and anger welled up inside of me; compassion on the boy and his family who were being pressed down by this trial, and anger at Satan for his malice.

We began to pray. Those close enough laid their hands on the boy as we prayed. Others stood at the door. One after another we prayed and resisted the devil on behalf of the family. When we were finished praying, there was a different atmosphere in the van. The family thanked us and left. We went back to our meeting.

Later, Leon told me that that evening was a turning point. His son's situation did not resolve immediately, but from that point on, it increasingly got better.

I began this chapter by pointing out that parents need to be alert to the spiritual conflict on behalf of their children. We do this by how we model the use of the means of grace for them, and by training them to make use of those means themselves. We are also alert on their behalf in our praying. There is one other way in which our alertness to the spiritual conflict around them expresses itself.

We parents must use our discernment on our children's behalf while they are maturing and learning discernment themselves. This applies to what books, videos, movies, and online entertainment we allow them to be exposed to. Any overt references to the demonic realm, even if supposedly only meant as a story or art form, are dangerous. Storylines involving sorcerers, witches, spells, mediums, and things like these, put the child's curiosity on the doorstep of the unseen realm. Once on the doorstep, it is easy to go through the door.

The Lord's opposition to actual witchcraft and sorcery is strong and unwavering. All practices associated with intentionally reaching out to the unseen realm are forbidden—even called abominations.

> There shall not be found among you anyone who... practices divination or tells fortunes or interprets omens, or a sorcerer or a charmer or a medium or a necromancer or one who inquires of the dead, for whoever does these things is an abomination to the Lord.[113]

If we expose our children to stories that contain such practices, we must do so with great caution and have some overriding purpose in mind, along with a good dose of parental editing and instruction. To allow our children to immerse themselves unsupervised in the latest best-selling novel or scary movie or online viral video that is filled with what the Bible calls abominations, and that can prompt them to experiment with the unseen realm in real life, is worse than negligent parenting. It is foolish irresponsibility in the face of an enemy who is trying to devour our children.

Some of the most touching stories from the life of Christ involve parents coming to him on behalf of children whom Satan had attacked. A Syrophoenician woman heard that the Jewish miracle-working Rabbi was in her Gentile neighborhood. Her concern for her daughter pushed her across cultural boundaries, and she walked in uninvited to a Jewish all-male gathering, humbled herself before Jesus, and persevered in pleading for the deliverance of her

---

[113] Deuteronomy 18:10 – 12.

daughter.[114] Undoubtedly, her relief and gratitude were enormous when she finally heard his words, "Go your way, the demon has left your daughter."[115] Likewise, the father of a little boy who was seized by an evil spirit pleaded first with Jesus' disciples, and then with Jesus himself.[116] Finally, "Jesus rebuked the unclean spirit and healed the boy, and gave him back to this father."[117] What joy to receive back from Jesus a child who you thought you had lost to the devil!

Parents, I realize that the insidious readiness of the enemy to attack your children is unsettling. But knowing that Jesus is ready to help parents should overcome your fear. He is ready to help every parent who goes to him on behalf of their child's deliverance from Satan. Go to Jesus for your children. He delights to answer.

---

[114] Mark 7:24 – 30.
[115] Mark 7:29.
[116] Matthew 17:14 – 19; Mark 9:14 – 19; Luke 9:37 – 42.
[117] Luke 9:42.

15

EVIL PEOPLE

O Lord my God, in you do I take refuge; save me from all my pursuers and deliver me.

King David

We know that we do not wrestle against flesh and blood. People are not our ultimate enemies. Nevertheless, there are times when the demonic realm has so influenced a person, and they have so cooperated with that influence, that he or she has become a channel of evil directed towards us. Paul warned Timothy of one such person.

> Alexander the coppersmith did me great harm; the Lord will repay him according to his deeds. Beware of him yourself, for he strongly opposed our message.[118]

There are some people who we need to view differently from others. They are spiritually dangerous to us. Although we are all

---

[118] 2 Timothy 4:14 – 15.

sinners and undeserving of God's love, some people are actually
deserving of being called *wicked* or *evil*. Notice, in Paul's words to
the Thessalonians, how he referred to some people as evil and that
he asserted that it was Satan who was behind those evil people's
intent to harm.

> Finally, brothers, pray for us, that the word of the
> Lord may speed ahead and be honored, as happened
> among you, and that we may be delivered from
> wicked and evil men. For not all have faith. But the
> Lord is faithful. He will establish you and guard
> you against the evil one.[119]

You begin to suspect that you are dealing with an evil person
when you compare what Jesus has told us of the intent and nature
of the devil with that person's actions and words, as well as the
consequences that person produces in your life. When destruction
and lies are persistently perpetrated on you from a particular person,
there is a good chance that he or she is being used as an instrument
of the devil. Sometimes it seems that the person is not doing this
intentionally, but interactions with him or her are laden with negative
spiritual consequence. At other times the person is actually targeting
you, and his or her ill will is tied to the fact that you profess to be a
follower of Christ. In either case, behind the scenes the evil one is
using that person.

Many times we can protect ourselves merely by avoiding such
an individual. At other times, the person is connected to us through
family or work or neighborhood relationships, and we cannot
completely disassociate ourselves from him or her. In such cases, we
do what Paul did when he wrote to the Thessalonians; we pray for
deliverance and lean on God for protection.

---

[119]   2 Thessalonians 3:1 – 3.

I believe that we have been given help in the Scriptures concerning how to pray when we are in such circumstances and that we find this help in the imprecatory psalms.

"To imprecate" is to invoke or call down judgment upon an enemy. Many of the psalms were composed in desperate circumstances in which evil people were oppressing the people of God. Contained in these psalms are prayers for calamity to fall on their enemies.[120] Present-day American Christians have a hard time knowing what to do with these psalms. Several questions come to mind. Aren't we taught to love our enemies, and even to pray for them? Do we not see that even a violent enemy of the gospel like Saul can be converted? Doesn't the Bible say that we were once all enemies of God? Isn't persecution to be expected in this life?[121] These questions all point to important Scripture passages and remind us that the proper use of the imprecatory psalms requires careful thinking. But our hesitancy in the face of the imprecatory psalms also points to a set of culturally-conditioned attitudes. Such attitudes mitigate against the acceptance of the biblical descriptions of God's hatred of, and antagonism towards, sin and evil.

I believe that the way the psalmist imprecatorily prays can be utilized for our praying when we are under satanic attack that presents itself in and through a person. What do I mean? I point your attention to Psalms 55, 7, and 36. I suggest that you read each of them in its entirety before reading my corresponding comments.

Psalm 55

Throughout this psalm we see expressions of the deep emotional toll that a particular person and his associates were having on David. "I am restless in my complaint and I moan." (v.2) "My heart is in anguish within me; the terrors of death have fallen upon me. Fear and trembling come upon me, and horror overwhelms me."

---

[120] Examples of imprecatory psalms are Psalms 7, 35, 55, 58, 59, 69, 79, 109, 137 and 139.

[121] Luke 6:27 – 28; Acts 9:1 – 18; Colossians 1:21 – 22; Acts 14:22.

(vv.4 – 5) His stress level was so high that all he wanted to do was get out of the situation. "Oh, that I had wings like a dove! I would fly away and be at rest." (v.6)

Perhaps you have felt this way. If so, you are not alone. On more than one occasion, I too, have experienced these thoughts and feelings. That is what drew me to these psalms for help.

What was it that this person was doing to David? He and his allies were "making noise." David wrote, "They drop trouble upon me, and in anger they bear a grudge against me." (v.3) They also spread violence and fraud. (vv.9,11)

To make matters worse, the ringleader of all this trouble was a former friend. "For it is not an enemy who taunts me—then I could bear it; it is not an adversary who deals insolently with me—then I could hide from him. But it is you, a man, my equal, my companion, my familiar friend. We used to take sweet counsel together; within God's house we walked in the throng." (vv.12 – 14)

Amid such distressing circumstances, David resorts to prayer, and it is when he does so that we see the vigor with which he asks God to intervene. He prays, "O Lord, divide their tongues." (v.9) And then he prays, "Let death steal over them; let them go down to Sheol alive; for evil is in their dwelling place and in their heart." (v.15)

How do I take that example and use it in my own life? When someone is bearing a grudge against me undeservedly and is making noise with threats of violence—when they are continually dropping trouble on me, even after I have sought to make peace and reconciliation, I ask God to "divide their tongue." It is their words that are bringing hurt and fear. So I lift the prayer of David out of Psalm 55, and put it into my prayers. Satan is using the tongue of the person, so I fight back by asking God to divide the person's tongue.

As for David's prayer that the person would die, I will discuss that a little later.

Psalm 7

In this psalm David makes it clear that he feels attacked, and that the attack is coming through particular individuals. "O Lord my God, in you do I take refuge; save me from all my pursuers and deliver me, lest like a lion they tear my soul apart, rending it in pieces, with none to deliver." (vv.1 – 2) It is interesting to me that he describes them as "pursuers." Have you ever been bothered by someone who, despite your attempts to make peace, just will not let you alone? That is the same experience of David. Evil is pursuing, and it is centralized in a person.

That person's words and actions resemble the devil's. "Behold, the wicked man conceives evil and is pregnant with mischief and gives birth to lies. He makes a pit, digging it out." (v.14) He or she is lying and plotting harm against you.

So what does David do? He starts with himself. He examines himself before the Lord to make sure he has done no wrong. "O Lord my God, if I have done this, if there is wrong in my hands, if I have repaid my friend with evil or plundered my enemy without cause, let the enemy pursue my soul and overtake it, and let him trample my life to the ground and lay my glory in the dust." (vv.3 – 5)

There is an important lesson here. When involved in interpersonal conflict, we must humbly admit and repent of any wrong we have done. When Satan attacks us through another person, we may not be responsible for the attack, but we are responsible for how we respond. Rarely do we respond without some shortcoming of our own. David shows us what to do. We own up to our own fault in the situation and then move on to pray against unrighteousness.

David leans on the character of God and prays without hesitation against his tormentor. He believes God is just and that he hates and punishes sin. Therefore, his one prayer in this psalm is: "Oh, let the evil of the wicked come to an end, and may you establish the righteous— you who test the minds and hearts, O righteous God!" (v.9)

He expects God to answer. "Behold, the wicked man...makes a pit, digging it out, and falls into the hole that he has made. His mischief returns upon his own head, and on his own skull his violence descends." (vv.14 – 16)

How do I take this example and apply it to my own life? First, I examine myself and ask forgiveness for any sin on my part. Then I pray that God will cause the evil person to "fall into his own pit" and that God will turn around his plots and have the evil fall on him.[122]

I have learned that there is strength to this kind of praying. We mustn't be quick to do so, but when the situation calls for it, we are encouraged by these psalms to beseech God to act in power against the evil person.

Psalm 36

This psalm begins with a disturbing description of evil people. Although disturbing, it helps us to see more clearly the kind of people about whom we are speaking. The evil person is not merely an unbeliever who is minding his or her own business. This is someone set against God and his people.

> Transgression speaks to the wicked deep in his heart; there is no fear of God before his eyes. For he flatters himself in his own eyes that his iniquity cannot be found out and hated. The words of his mouth are trouble and deceit; he has ceased to act

---

[122] There is a rhyme made of verses 15 – 16 which captures the meaning well. This is found on page 115 of William Plumer's rich commentary, *Psalms: A Critical and Expository Commentary with Doctrinal and Practical Remarks.*
"He digs a ditch and delves it deep,
In hope to hurt his brother;
But he shall fall into the pit
That he digged up for other.
Thus wrong returneth to the hurt
Of him in whom it bred;
And all the mischief that he wrought,
Shall fall upon his head."

wisely and do good. He plots trouble while on his bed; he sets himself in a way that is not good; he does not reject evil. (vv.1 – 4)

When persons like that have you in their sights, you must seek God's protection and fight back with prayer.

The entire second half of this psalm is all about God. Instead of giving details about his own distress, as he did in Psalm 55, David extols the love, righteousness, mercy, and generous heart of God. He asks that God continue his loving care over him and then finally makes one request about his enemy. "Let not the foot of arrogance come upon me, nor the hand of the wicked drive me away." (v.11) That was his request. Then, in a confident statement of what he believed God would do, he ends the psalm saying, "There the evildoers lie fallen; they are thrust down, unable to rise." (v.12) In essence, he prayed that God would thrust down his enemy.

Granted, this kind of prayer is not always needed, but when it is, I have learned to pray, with trembling, that God would thrust down the one who is being used by Satan.

But how far down? This is where the weight of other verses bears down upon me and forces a balance. Do I pray for the person's death?

No. I lift phrases from the imprecatory psalms that seem most fitting and pray them against the person who is steadfastly being used by the evil one. I ask things like, "Divide his tongue!" and "Cause him to fall into his own pit!" But I remember that Jesus rebuked two of his disciples for too eagerly desiring to call down judgment on others.[123] I also remember that in Psalm 7:12 David

---

123 Luke 9:51 – 56. "When the days drew near for him to be taken up, he set his face to go to Jerusalem. And he sent messengers ahead of him, who went and entered a village of the Samaritans, to make preparations for him. But the people did not receive him, because his face was set toward Jerusalem. And when his disciples James and John saw it, they said, 'Lord, do you want us to tell fire to come down from heaven and

said, "If a man does not repent, God will whet his sword." I must pray for the person's repentance even as I pray for God to rise up and quell the evil. And so, I've found myself praying at times, "Lord, bring this person to repentance. But if this person will not repent, thrust him aside! How far down you thrust him is up to you, but I ask that you put him aside, so that evil will not prevail."

I have seen people who were so angry at certain Christians that their veins stood out from their necks and their eyes bulged while they spewed curses, threats, and lies. In one case, this kind of behavior was repeated over a period of months. The Christians who were targeted with this hatred were initially struck with fear and confusion. After extended time in the kind of prayer I have described here, the same belligerent ones, when in the presence of the Christians, went completely silent, and on one occasion, even turned and fled. Nothing was said aloud or done to the angry ones, but behind the scenes there had been aggressive imprecatory praying. God answered the Christians' prayers!

Evil people exist, and Satan uses them against us. The imprecatory psalms give us examples of how to pray against them. In one of those psalms, David turned his attention to those of us who would come after him. He uses his difficult experience to coach us. We would do well to follow his advice:

> But I call to God, and the Lord will save me. Evening and morning and at noon I utter my complaint and moan, and he hears my voice. He redeems my soul in safety from the battle that I wage, for many are arrayed against me. God will give ear and humble them, he who is enthroned from of old…Cast your burden on the Lord, and he will sustain you; he will never permit the righteous to be moved.[124]

---

consume them?' But he turned and rebuked them. And they went on to another village."

[124]   Psalm 55:16 – 19, 22.

16

EVANGELISM AND THE UNSEEN REALM

Whenever the gospel comes with Spirit and power this preaching quickly gives an alarm to hell, and raises all manner of opposition against it. Satan is the god of this world. No prince on earth is more jealous of the revolt of his subjects than he, and he stirs himself up when the gospel comes to dethrone him.

John Flavel

We have become accustomed to describing an individual's resistance to the gospel in terms of the effect that sin has had on him or her. We understand that apart from any work of the Spirit of God the mind is darkened, the heart is cold, and the person's will is set against Christ.[125] It is true that all of this is due to sin, but there is another complicating factor: the devil.

---

[125] 1 Corinthians 2:14; John 3:19; Romans 8:5 – 8.

> And even if our gospel is veiled, it is veiled only to those who are perishing. In their case the god of this world has blinded the minds of the unbelievers, to keep them from seeing the light of the gospel of the glory of Christ, who is the image of God....For God, who said, "Let light shine out of darkness," has shone in our hearts to give the light of the knowledge of the glory of God in the face of Jesus Christ.[126]

Notice that in the case of unbelievers there is a satanic element to their lack of comprehension. The "god of this world" is actively trying to keep them from understanding the gospel. We must not be naïve about the nature of evangelism—when we engage in evangelism, we are in direct conflict with Satan.

In the above Scripture passage, we also see that conversion is a supernatural event. It took God's power to create light in the midst of darkness. In the same way, it takes the mighty power of God to shine into blinded minds and overcome both the effects of sin and the work of the devil. When we involve ourselves in evangelism, it ought to be with the prayer that God uses our efforts to do that divine work in the unbeliever.

We reason with unbelievers about the gospel, aiming at their understanding. We testify to them, warning them of the consequences of their unbelief. We persuade them, aiming for a decision of their will.[127] But we do all this knowing that we cannot actually cause them to understand, feel the necessary heart change, and decide for Christ. It is only God who causes those things to happen. Nevertheless, he uses our words in the process. And make

---

[126]   2 Corinthians 4:3 – 6.

[127]   These three aspects of evangelism are all seen in Acts 18:4 – 5 where the words, "reasoned," "persuaded," and "testified" are used to describe what Paul did in Corinth.

no mistake about it, as this process of drawing people to Christ is taking place, there is a conflict with the evil one.

Be alert when involved in evangelism

Evangelism *is* spiritual warfare. Knowing that, we must be aware of the source of the opposition to our efforts. I have noticed over the years that, whenever there is a concerted effort by a church to evangelize, there inevitably arise those who oppose. In one case of which I am aware, a church had a booth at the local county fair for years. When they decided to emphasize evangelism, their long-standing permission was revoked. Churches can do all sorts of ministries that meet various needs in the community and find help, and even encouragement, from the local authorities. But when the presentation of the gospel becomes the centerpiece of their efforts, opposition almost always comes.

While opposition comes through people, there is often also a proliferation of unusual events or occurrences that distract and hinder. Malfunctioning machinery, injuries, important items lost— all this and more, and all with a frequency or unusual nature, which begs the question, why is all this happening to us at this time?

Early in our missionary years, my wife and I were living in a small village. The people in that place were unevangelized. Their entire history was gospel-less. After having established relationships with the villagers and their leaders, the time came that my African co-worker and I sensed God's leading to have an outdoor, public presentation of the gospel. We made special plans for guest speakers, invited VIPs, and spread the word to all the surrounding villages. Finally, we were on the eve of the meetings. That night, after putting each of our children to bed, my wife and I were quietly chatting in the kitchen. Within my peripheral vision I noticed something moving on the kitchen wall. I turned to look. It was a stream of ants, locally called Siafu. Siafu travel in the hundreds of thousands and eat everything in their path. They have large pinchers and insatiable appetites. They swarm over their prey until you cannot see anything except a mass of ants. Underneath that pulsing black heap, the unfortunate target is killed and eaten. They eat other insects and any animals that can't escape. Chickens and goats have been eaten down to the bone. In tragic cases, even unattended infants have perished.

Our infant daughter was in a room along the same wall. Her two siblings were asleep in a neighboring room. The ants poured over the top of the kitchen wall like a black waterfall. We ran into the kids' rooms and saw that the ants were descending over their walls too. We grabbed all the children and shouted a warning to our guests. We made our way through the house to safety outside. There wasn't a room without Siafu in it.

That house was used by missionaries for almost two decades after that incident. Neither before that night nor ever again did Siafu invade, but on the eve of the first outdoor proclamation of the gospel of Jesus Christ among an unreached people, the Siafu came like a flood. Only a person raised with a Western, anti-supernatural education would believe that this was a coincidence.

This example may seem dramatic, but in principle it occurs over and over again. Churches and individuals make plans to share the gospel, and then they find themselves besought with distractions and hindrances.

Another common form of hindrance is interpersonal conflict among the Christians doing the evangelism. I've seen it many times. Christians who normally get along with each other in other circumstances become irritated with each other when working on an evangelistic enterprise. The conflicts escalate, and often the leader is using his or her time and energy as a mediator, mending relationships rather than focusing on evangelism.

We see the opposition on a personal level too. Why such hesitancy to share the gospel with a friend or co-worker? Why such difficulty in bringing up the topic of spiritual things with your neighbor with whom you've enjoyed so many good conversations about other topics? Just as in any temptation, the temptation to stay quiet rather than witness could merely be a factor of the world and the flesh. But sometimes there is a demonic element, especially since evangelism is such a direct confrontation of Satan's domain.

We need to be aware of the satanic resistance associated with sharing the gospel with unbelievers.

Practice aggressive praying during times of evangelism.

What do we do with this awareness? As is the case with so much else that is associated with conflict in the spiritual realm, we pray.

First, we pray against the satanic element of the opposition we are facing. We can do this ahead of time as we are preparing for evangelistic events. We ask God to keep the evil one at bay, and if so prompted by the Spirit, we may resist the devil and order him out of our preparations.

If opposition is presenting itself once evangelism has begun, we can address the unseen source of the troubling occurrences. In group prayer we worship the Lord, ask him for help, and then momentarily turn our attention to the enemy while one person says something like, *"Satan, in the name and authority of Jesus Christ, we reject your attempts to interfere with the gospel being proclaimed. We resist you and order you away from us. We tear down your plans that you have against us, for the Word of God says, 'For the weapons of our warfare are not of the flesh but have divine power to destroy strongholds.'"*[128] Such a rebuke of Satan can even be more specific, naming the particular occurrences or the trouble. After someone voices this rebuke, the others all say "Amen!" and continue in prayer. Again, the object is not to have a discussion with the evil one, nor to linger on that aspect, but to resist firmly and with authority, and then move on.

That night when the Siafu were pouring into our house by the hundreds of thousands, we had an African evangelist sleeping in one of our rooms. We woke him up, and we all took refuge from the ants. It was obvious to him what was behind this occurrence, and he prayed using Isaiah 54:17. At one point he broke off from prayer and

---

[128]   2 Corinthians 10:4.

addressed the devil, "Satan, we rebuke you away from us. You are using the Siafu, but God says, 'No weapon that is fashioned against you shall succeed,' and so your plans will fail. We resist you and order you away from us and from the gospel meetings tomorrow." The ants eventually left, and in the meetings the next day, a man put his faith in Christ. He was later baptized, eventually becoming the first person of that entire people group to serve as a church deacon. In all the years since that day, as more people believed and the church spread to several villages, that man proved to be a steady, faithful, vital part of the movement of God among his people. Hallelujah!

Let me offer one more piece of advice. My wife and I learned the hard way that when our missionary team or our church steps out on an evangelistic endeavor, it is time for us as a family to "circle the wagons." I've already discussed how Satan attacks children. In our early days, we noticed that our children often bore the brunt of the attacks during evangelistic efforts. Freak accidents and unusual situations would pepper the days and nights of our outreach. We learned to shorten the leash on our kids. We did not grow afraid and quit evangelism. Rather, we grew more serious about our adversary, took more precautions, and emphasized evangelism even harder. We would not allow our children to go too far from us or to venture into anything that risked physical injury. Instead, we pulled them in tighter, involved them in the evangelism itself, and prayed against the enemy's attempts to hurt them. In our later missionary years, we saw a lot of victory with this approach.

Second, we pray against Satan's attempt to intimidate us from speaking. If you are suspecting opposition from the enemy as you attempt to witness, pause and pray. Ask God for help. Then momentarily address the enemy by saying something like this, "*Satan, in the name and authority of Jesus Christ, I resist your attempts to keep me from witnessing to _____. Be gone from me, for the Word of God says, 'For I am not ashamed of the gospel, for it is the power of God for salvation to everyone who believes, to the Jew first and also to the Greek.*'"[129] Then turn your attention back to God and finish your praying. Whether in group evangelistic endeavors or personal attempts, when we are opposed by the evil one, we have every right to stand in Christ and resist.

Third, we pray against Satan's hindrance of the unsaved to believe.

Scripture should shape how we pray for our unbelieving friends and family. The Bible teaches us that no one comes to Christ "unless the Father draws him,"[130] and so we lift those words from the Bible and ask God to draw the person to Christ. Likewise, Scripture says that the Holy Spirit convicts the world of "sin and righteousness and judgment,"[131] and so we pray that God would convict the person of sin. Wherever the Bible speaks of the process of a person becoming a Christian, we can use that instruction to inform our praying for the unsaved.

With this in mind, we remember that we are told that "the god of this world has blinded the minds of the unbelievers, to keep them from seeing the light of the gospel."[132] And so we pray against the devil and his attempts to blind the minds of those to whom we are witnessing. This kind of prayer on behalf of unbelievers is an important addition to our arsenal as we participate with God in his work of saving people.

Keep presenting the gospel to the unsaved!

In addition to being aware of Satan's opposition and practicing aggressive prayer, we must not back down from evangelism itself. As I've already said, evangelism *is* spiritual warfare.

When the Apostle Paul was converted,[133] Jesus told him what God was saving him to do.

---

[129]　Romans 1:16.
[130]　John 6:44.
[131]　John 16:8.
[132]　2 Corinthians 4:4.
[133]　Acts 9:1 – 19.

> I have appeared to you for this purpose, to appoint
> you as a...witness...to open their eyes, so that they
> may turn from darkness to light and from the power
> of Satan to God.[134]

As God saves people, he is turning them from darkness to light. You are directly engaged in opposing the devil when you are sharing the gospel with an unbeliever.

You can take the battle to the enemy by witnessing to all those in your life who have not yet believed in Christ. I urge you, don't let anything keep you quiet. Share the gospel with others, for by so doing, you will be participating in God's victory over the evil one.

The Apostle Paul includes our witnessing in his list of spiritual armor. It shows up in the list as the boots that the soldier wears into battle: "And, as shoes for your feet, having put on the readiness given by the gospel of peace."[135] The wording of that verse draws attention to *readiness*. Readiness for what? For the proclamation of the gospel of peace. May the Lord find us faithful in wearing the "gospel boots" of our spiritual armor—speaking about Christ to unbelievers whenever we have an opportunity.

The shortest parable.

Some Bible scholars call Mark 3:27 the shortest parable of Jesus. Even though short, it contains important information for us as we grapple with the unseen opposition to evangelism.

> But no one can enter a strong man's house and
> plunder his goods, unless he first binds the strong
> man. Then indeed he may plunder his house.[136]

---

134   Acts 26:16 – 18.
135   Ephesians 6:15.
136   The account within which this parable is told is found in Mark 3:22 – 30.

Jesus uttered these words in response to the Jewish scribes who were accusing him of being possessed by the prince of demons. This was their explanation for his success in casting out evil spirits. After stressing that such a scenario would mean that Satan's kingdom was divided against itself, he told them the real reason for his success. He was stronger than Satan and able to neutralize Satan in order to rescue people from his bondage.

Unbelievers are the goods that are locked up in Satan's house. Satan has tremendous power to keep those people under his control. Jesus has entered Satan's house, and by his death, resurrection, and ascension, he has bound Satan. Salvation is God's work, yet he is pleased to use us in it. We are required to reckon Jesus' victory over Satan as true, and to act upon that truth. We resist Satan and speak in Christ's name, trusting in Christ's victory, presenting the gospel to people trapped in Satan's house. Jesus then manifests his victory over Satan by bringing the salvation he accomplished on the cross into the hearts of unbelievers. Our thrill is that we get to participate in this process and see the Lord work!

One of Isaiah's prophecies is echoed in Jesus' shortest parable.

> Can the prey be taken from the mighty, or the captives of a tyrant be rescued? For thus says the Lord: "Even the captives of the mighty shall be taken, and the prey of the tyrant be rescued, for I will contend with those who contend with you, and I will save your children. ... Then all flesh shall know that I am the Lord your Savior, and your Redeemer, the Mighty One of Jacob."[137]

Each time an unbeliever puts his or her faith in Jesus Christ, it is evidence of Jesus binding the strong man, and one more affirmation that Jesus alone is Lord. One day all flesh will confess that Jesus is Lord. Until then, as we fulfill our responsibility to be witnesses, Satan's work is thwarted, and God receives the glory that is his due.

---

[137]   Isaiah 49:24 – 26.

17

RENOUNCEMENT

For the grace of God has appeared, bringing salvation for all people, training us to renounce ungodliness and worldly passions, and to live self-controlled, upright, and godly lives in the present age.

Paul the Apostle

The dictionary gives a three-part definition of the word "renounce."

1. To give up or put aside voluntarily.
2. To give up by formal declaration.
3. To repudiate or disown.

Depending upon what sin we have engaged in or the avenue through which evil spirits have come our way, it is possible that there is a need for us to deliberately declare our repudiation of particular evils. Look again at Acts 19.

> Also many of those who were now believers came, confessing and divulging their practices. And a number of those who had practiced magic arts brought their books together and burned them in the sight of all. And they counted the value of them and found it came to fifty thousand pieces of silver. So the word of the Lord continued to increase and prevail mightily.[138]

The act of destroying the books was an important step in the Christians' battle with the enemy. By destroying the books, they were renouncing their involvement in the magic arts.

There were two important facets to this renouncement. First, their own wills were involved. Second, there was a tangible break with past practices.

Their own wills. No one threw the books into the fire for them. The ones who had used the books brought the books and burned the books. This is an important facet of experiencing freedom from the oppression of the evil one. Some people who have a past that included willful participation in activities that opened them up to the devil's attacks expect to be delivered solely on the basis of other people's prayers. While it is true that there is strength when others pray for us, it is also true that if a person has not engaged his or her own will in denouncing and rejecting past involvement, there will always remain a foothold for the devil.

A tangible break with past practices. Sometimes there are physical objects that were used in past sinful practices. These objects need to be disposed of—even destroyed if possible. This needs to be done in the name of Christ and as an expression of the person's firm decision to forsake the sinful practices and follow Christ more fully.

At other times, however, even if there is no physical object, there can be a need for a purposeful rejection of the sin. For example, a

---

[138] Acts 19:18 – 20.

man who has repeatedly gone to those who use tarot cards needs to renounce this practice verbally—to make it "official" before God and Satan—in order to close all the doors that he had opened to the evil one. He has no objects to burn in a fire, but he has a renouncement to make.

Whether there are objects to be disposed of or not, the person making the renouncement can proceed in the following way. He begins by confessing his sin to the Lord, claiming his forgiveness because of the blood of Christ, surrendering his life again to the Lordship of Christ, and then saying something like this:

Lord, right now I renounce (here he mentions the sinful practice). I reject that as sinful and say that I will never do it again. [If there is an object, he burns or disposes of it at this time.] I reject any spirit associated with that evil (and that object). And I say to Satan—The Lord rebuke you from me! Any advantage that you gained in my life through this sin, I take back from you! For the Word of God says, "For the weapons of our warfare are mighty before God for the destruction of fortresses." So, in the name of Christ, I destroy any fortress you built up against me by my involvement in those things.

Then he turns his attention back to the Lord, worships him, and asks him for a fresh filling of the Holy Spirit. He has now renounced the evil practices. His prayer and renouncement has accomplished what the people in Acts 19 accomplished by burning the books.

The following list includes practices and involvements that have the very real potential of opening a person up to demonic influence.[139]

Ouija board. Table lifting. Speaking in a trance. Automatic writing. Telepathy. Inviting interaction with ghosts or spirits. Clairvoyance. Vampirism. Fortune-telling. Tarot cards. Palm-reading. Divination. Dependence upon astrology. Hypnosis. Magic

---

[139]   This is a slight alteration of Neil Anderson's list. For his complete list see page 245 of his very helpful book, *The Bondage Breaker.*

charms. Mental suggestion. Black and white magic. Fetishism. Witchcraft. Voodoo. Playing Charlie-Charlie. Reiki Therapy.

If you have a history of involvement in any of these practices, or another similar practice, I urge you to get on your knees before the Lord and renounce that past. Make it official before God and Satan. Use the pattern that I gave you above and insert your sinful practices into those sentences. If you need help, find someone in your church who can be present with you as you make your renouncement.

Evil spirits that stay in family lines. I know of no Bible verse that explicitly describes evil spirits staying within families and moving from one generation to another. Nevertheless, there is much evidence from life and ministry that such a thing happens. I and many others have seen situations in which a presence of evil attaches itself to someone because of some door that an ancestor opened to the demonic realm. Whether it was a parent, grandparent, or someone farther up the family line, an ancestor had been afflicted with an evil spirit, and upon that person's death it appears that the spirit moved to a descendant.

This attack of the enemy can be thwarted by renouncing the sins of your ancestor and rejecting the evil spirit's attempt to trouble you. There is no need to despair. You can break the spirit's connection to you in the name of Christ.

Here is an example of how you could word such a renouncement. The first sentence is only used if you know the details about your ancestor.

I confess that what my (parent, grandparent, etc.) did was sinful, and I reject it. I reject any spirit associated with my (parent, grandparent, etc.) and that intends to work evil against me. I claim the blood of Christ for my own forgiveness and say that I believe in Jesus Christ and that God has delivered me from the domain of darkness and transferred me to the kingdom of his beloved Son.[140] Right now, I address any evil spirit

---

[140] Colossians 1:13.

assigned to me coming from my (parent, grandparent, etc.). I break any bond between me and you, and I resist and reject you in Jesus' name, for the Word of God says, "Resist the devil and he will flee from you!"

As I have said before, this addressing of the evil one needs to be couched in prayer focused on the Lord. Worship the Lord before and after such a renouncement.

Gigi's Story

I was in my 40's when this happened. I lived in the Northeast and my parents lived in the South—hundreds of miles away. My father died. Of course, I went to the funeral and all my siblings were there. After the family gatherings, I traveled home. That was when I began to sense something wrong in my house. It never felt like this before or after. My husband and my children didn't seem to sense it, but I definitely felt it. I didn't really know what it was, but at times I would walk into a room and feel something dark. There was a presence of evil—something that was making me uneasy and even afraid. I don't come from a church that talks about evil spirits, and I hadn't been taught anything about them. Our pastor never mentioned things like that. So, I don't even know where I got the idea of what to do. Maybe it was just the Holy Spirit? Anyway, one day when my husband was at work and my children were in school, I walked around the whole house praying. I asked God for help,

and I told any evil that it was not welcome in
our house and that it must leave in Jesus' name.
The evil presence in my home ended that day!

Gigi did not have much coaching or biblical teaching, but God
led her and honored her faith. The bond was broken with whatever
spirit came her way after her father's death.

Whether an evil spirit comes your way because of one of your
ancestors or because of your own sinful involvement in occult
practices, Jesus can set you free. Part of the process of experiencing
that freedom will be a clear confession of any sin that you have
contributed to the situation and a definitive renouncement of the
evil. One of the wonders of God's grace is that when we confess and
forsake evil, we find Him ready to forgive and help.

> Seek the Lord while he may be found; call upon him
> while he is near; let the wicked forsake his way, and
> the unrighteous man his thoughts; let him return
> to the Lord, that he may have compassion on him,
> and to our God, for he will abundantly pardon.[141]

---

[141]   Isaiah 55:6 – 7.

18

DISTINGUISH
THE VOICES

*The devil shapes himself to the characteristics
of all men. If he meet with a proud man, or a
prodigal, then he makes himself a flatterer; if a
covetous man, then he comes with a reward in
his hand. He has an apple for Eve, a grape for
Noah, a change of clothes for Gehazi, a bag for
Judas. He can dish out his food for all palates.*
William Jenkyn

Jesus is called the Good Shepherd. The roots of that title are seen
in John 10. I give you, below, a portion of that chapter, but as you
read it, I want you to look for what is often missed. This portion of
Scripture tells us something about our enemy, as well as something
about our Shepherd.

Truly, truly, I say to you, he who does not enter
the sheepfold by the door but climbs in by another

way, that man is a thief and a robber. But he who enters by the door is the shepherd of the sheep. To him the gatekeeper opens. The sheep hear his voice, and he calls his own sheep by name and leads them out. When he has brought out all his own, he goes before them, and the sheep follow him, for they know his voice. A stranger they will not follow, but they will flee from him, for they do not know the voice of strangers.[142]

There are two different sources of the messages that come our way—the voice of the shepherd and the voice of the stranger. Both voices call to the sheep. The stranger, of course, is Satan. He calls to us, broadcasting untrue and harmful thoughts our way. As Christians we must grow in our ability to discern the enemy's voice so as to reject the thoughts that he is trying to get us to believe.

He speaks to us through the world in which we live. The corruption of our society and culture sends messages our way through many mouthpieces. These mouthpieces can be actual mouths— people with whom we interact who are speaking untruth to us. But the messages can also come by various media that propagate people's thoughts. Books, movies, internet, TV, theater…the various kinds of media are many, but the principle is the same—Satan uses people to broadcast error our way.

Those who broadcast error may be unwittingly cooperating with Satan as they put falsehood into our minds, or in some cases they are actually evil and are doing it with intent. Either way, it is the "voice of strangers" trying to work deception and destruction in our lives.

We've already seen that Satan is the father of lies, and that which he speaks is always false.[143] When we accept a message that has come either directly or indirectly from him, that means we have accepted a

---

[142] John 10:1 – 5.
[143] John 8:44.

falsehood. If we accept it, we begin to believe it and eventually make decisions based upon it. At this point the devil's strategy is working. We are listening to the stranger's voice rather than our shepherd's, and it is leading us towards destruction.

Proverbs teaches us that "a man without self-control is like a city broken into and left without walls."[144] That image of a person being protected by surrounding walls, combined with the idea of differing voices in John 10, produces the illustration below.

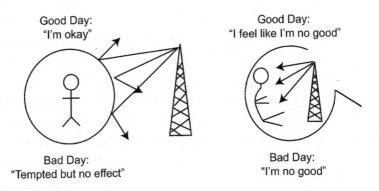

Good Day:
"I'm okay"

Good Day:
"I feel like I'm no good"

Bad Day:
"Tempted but no effect"

Bad Day:
"I'm no good"

In the illustration, the circle on the left represents the Christian who is living in a protected condition. The transmitting tower represents Satan, who broadcasts lies toward the Christian. Let me allow Rob Black, a gifted counselor, explain the illustration.

> The Proverbs verse likens us to a city with walls of protection around us. This speaks of the secure state of the Christian, not exempt from troubles, but resilient in the face of them when walking closely with God. In contrast is the one who "has no control over his spirit" and is vulnerable and without protection from God....The two circles in the diagram represent the protected and

---

144   Proverbs 25:28.

unprotected conditions. John 10:1 – 5 distinguishes the two message sources, the Shepherd and the Enemy. When the believer is walking in faith and obedience, the Enemy's efforts are "at a distance." When the believer allows sin to reign, the protection is compromised and the attacks come up close.[145]

I've seen the truth of this illustration in my own experience and in the lives of others I've been privileged to help. Suggestions from the evil one come our way, such as, "*you* are no good," or "*you* are a failure," or "*you* will never amount to anything," or "*you* are only human—nobody's perfect," or "*you* are too weak—you can't do what God is asking." When we are walking with God these voices are easily recognized for what they are—lies. But when the walls are broken down and allowed to be in disrepair for a long time, the transmitting tower moves within the walls. Soon we are unaware that these thoughts are not our own. We are now thinking things like, "*I'm* no good," or "*I'm* a failure," or "*I* will never amount to anything," or "*I* am only human," or "*I'm* too weak." We've adopted Satan's suggestions as our own, forgetting that they originally came from outside of us. They now seem to be our own thoughts. We need to wake up and distinguish the voices!

We hear the voice of the Good Shepherd in Scripture. There he tells us truth such as, "In him you have been made complete,"[146] or "I can do all things through him who strengthens me,"[147] or "We are his workmanship, created in Christ Jesus for good works, which God prepared beforehand so that we would walk in them,"[148] or "No temptation has overtaken you but such as is common to man; and God is faithful, who will not allow you to be tempted beyond what you are able, but with the temptation will provide the way of escape also, so that

---

[145]   Rob Black, *Picture This: Diagrams to Make Scriptural Truths Clear* (published by author, 2014), 100.

[146]   Colossians 2:10.

[147]   Philippians 4:13.

[148]   Ephesians 2:10.

you will be able to endure it."[149] Accepting the Good Shepherd's truth, believing it, and making decisions based upon it, leads us away from destruction and towards life.

How do we protect ourselves from this strategy of the evil one?

The first aspect of our protection is our refusal to be naïve concerning all the messages that are sent our way. Paul said, "But I am afraid that as the serpent deceived Eve by his cunning, your thoughts will be led astray from a sincere and pure devotion to Christ."[150] The enemy starts with our minds. In order to lead us astray, he seeks to deceive. It is significant that Satan did not begin with Eve by trying to scare her but by trying to deceive her.

In my opinion, there is an appalling lack of discernment among many American Christians as to the voices to which they allow themselves to be exposed. I am not arguing for a retreat from our culture—that all Christians run and hide themselves from the world. We are the salt of the earth and need to be engaged in our local communities and the wider culture. But in our engagement we must use discernment. Our culture is filled with mouthpieces of the evil one, broadcasting untruth to us and to our children. Sometimes the messages are blatant and at other times subtle, but the voice is the same voice—that of the "stranger." What we watch and listen to contains many untrue messages. We need to seek the balance between involvement in the culture and careful spiritual protection of ourselves and our children. I am convinced that the prayer of the apostle Paul for the Philippian Christians is needed today for American Christians.

> And this I pray, that your love may abound still more
> and more in real knowledge and all discernment, so
> that you may approve the things that are excellent,
> in order to be sincere and blameless until the day

---

[149]   1 Corinthians 10:13.
[150]   2 Corinthians 11:3.

of Christ; having been filled with the fruit of righteousness which comes through Jesus Christ, to the glory and praise of God.[151]

The second aspect of our protection is the continual, regular involvement in the means of grace. I cannot overemphasize the importance of our Spirit-given discipline in availing ourselves of those means. The Word of God, prayer, fellowship, service, the ordinances, and the heart attitudes of trust and obedience—these are the means by which the "wall around the city" is built and maintained. As regards discerning the enemy's voice, our efforts at saturating our minds with the Word of God are crucial. It is truth that shines the spotlight on error and chases it away. To expect spiritual protection from the voice of the evil one while neglecting the means of grace is like expecting to be warm outside on a frigid winter day without wearing a coat. You cannot neglect the necessary means without suffering the consequences.

A third aspect of our protection concerns what to do when we realize that the walls are broken down. We come to understand that the transmitting tower is inside the walls. We have been believing lies. There has been some sin reigning in us, and it has opened us up to Satan's ploys. What to do now?

Now is time to do battle in prayer. There is a way to pray that breaks the back of sin patterns in our lives. I call it the Battle Prayer. Harold Burchett coached me in this kind of praying and I have found great relief from sin and Satan in its use.

---

[151] Philippians 1:9 – 11.

The Battle Prayer

This is how you practice the Battle Prayer. Kneel in prayer with your Bible. In your own words, using a strong voice, follow these steps:

A. **A**dmit the sin or sins by name. (1 John 1:9)

B. Claim the **B**lood of Christ, which cleanses the sins just named. Read aloud 1 John 1:7b.

C. **C**onfess Jesus Christ as Lord of all—the sin area as well as all other areas of your life. Now present everything to him—your stubborn will, troubled emotions, ambitions, mind, abilities, every faculty, and even your physical body—its members, desires and ailments. Make the dedication of Romans 12:1 – 2.

D. Take a **D**efinite, strong stand in the authority of the Lord Jesus Christ—the one you have just named as Lord. Use words of strength such as, "Lord, I choose Your way." Or, "I choose to believe your words." If there is an intense struggle with Satan, take your stand definitely (James 4:7) using such terms as, "I refuse to believe the lies of my enemy," or "I reject/ renounce this mood of despair," or "In the name of the Lord Jesus Christ, I order you, Satan, out!" Here you will need to read and affirm each truth taught in Colossians 1:13 – 14. Notice that two opposing authorities are mentioned, and thank God you are transferred and brought under the authority of the beloved Son. This wonderful transaction is accomplished by the blood redemption.

E. Exalt the Lord! Turn to thanksgiving, praising God item by item for many of his good deeds toward you—mention carefully the works of the Son, God's care as Father and the patient ministries of the Holy Spirit sustaining and comforting you. Include your family and material benefits. Do not look back into the swamp—look up to God. (Hebrews 13:15)

F. Ask for a new **F**illing of the Holy Spirit, so that you might be restored, refreshed, and strengthened to obey the next obligation that God puts in your path. (Ephesians 5:18)

You can remember the steps by A (admit), B (blood), C (confess), D (definite), E (exalt), F (filling).[152]

When the walls are broken down, they need to be repaired. The first step in that repair is employing the Battle Prayer—full repentance, restoration, consecration, renewed focus, and filling. The transmitting tower is thrown out and the repair has begun!

I began this chapter by reminding you of a special title of our Lord: The Good Shepherd. It is a wondrous truth that he knows us, calls to us, leads us, provides for us, and protects us. Our participation in his protection of us is neither complicated nor cumbersome. If we

---

[152] This is an adaptation of teaching found on page 31 of Harold Burchett's *Spiritual Life Studies*.

want to make it simple, let's say it like this: Jesus will protect you.
Don't listen to the strangers; listen to the shepherd.

> The thief comes only to steal and kill and destroy; I
> came that they may have life, and have it abundantly.
> I am the good shepherd; the good shepherd lays
> down His life for the sheep. He who is a hired hand,
> and not a shepherd, who is not the owner of the
> sheep, sees the wolf coming, and leaves the sheep
> and flees, and the wolf snatches them and scatters
> them. He flees because he is a hired hand and is not
> concerned about the sheep. I am the good shepherd,
> and I know My own and My own know Me, even
> as the Father knows Me and I know the Father; and
> I lay down My life for the sheep.[153]

---

[153] John 10:10 – 15 New American Standard, Updated Version.

19

YOU DON'T HAVE
TO FIGHT ALONE.

The conflict which the apostle has been speaking about is not just a single battle between the individual Christian and Satan, but also a war between the people of God and the powers of darkness. No soldier entering battle prays for himself alone, but for all his fellow soldiers also. They form one army, and the success of one is the success of all. In a similar way Christians are united as one army and therefore have a common cause, and each must pray for everyone else. Such is the communion of saints.

Charles Hodge

The United States Army once had a recruiting slogan, Army of One. The slogan didn't last long, and no one who has ever gone through basic training was surprised when it ended up in the trash bin. One of the first doctrines that gets drilled into new recruits' heads is that they will only succeed if they approach their mission together. Teamwork is absolutely vital to their success while in basic training and later when they are in combat.

So it is with us in our spiritual battle. Although we are often attacked when we are alone and therefore need to be equipped to resist the devil as an individual, the Lord has placed each one of us in his body and designed us all to be interdependent. There are four important reasons why you should allow the body of believers to share in your spiritual struggles.

There is power in united prayer.

The great majority of the examples of prayer that we see in the New Testament are examples of group prayer. We see this in the book of Acts and even notice that the instruction that we receive about prayer in the epistles is largely concerning groups of Christians praying together.[154] In many circles within American Christianity, the experience of Spirit-led group prayer is something found only in their history books. This is a terrible loss, and certainly does not help in the church's ability to stand firm amidst spiritual onslaughts. On the other hand, within a growing number of churches, there has been in recent years a noticeable re-emphasis and re-discovery of the power of group prayer. This movement to prioritize group prayer is an encouraging sign of hope for all of us who know our own weakness in the face of the enemy.

Because of the differences between New Testament Greek and our English, there are some nuances in the Scriptures that are easy for us to miss. For example, the famous passage on spiritual conflict in Ephesians 6 is addressed to Christians as a group rather than to individuals. In other words, when it says to "put on the whole armor of God, that you may be able to stand against the schemes of the devil,"[155] the command "put" is given to them as a group.

---

[154]　Applicable examples found in Acts 12:5; 2 Corinthians 1:11; 1 Timothy 2:8.

[155]　Ephesians 6:11.

Also, the "you" is plural—those of us with ties to Appalachia or the South would say "y'all." It is not addressed to an individual but to the group, and they are to obey it together. It is the same situation later in the passage, when Paul talks about prayer. We are told as a group to be "praying at all times in the Spirit, with all prayer and supplication."[156]

As the stories in this book have shown, often attacks occur when we are alone, and we must fend them off by ourselves. But in the case of prolonged attacks and intensely difficult situations, we need to ask others to join in with us. One of the main ways they do so is in their prayers.

There are some in the church who are gifted in discernment.

God has designed the local church to consist of various people with various divine enablements. No one of us has all the gifts. We need each other. As the passage below explains, we are each gifted for the sake of others in the body.

> Now there are varieties of gifts, but the same Spirit; and there are varieties of service, but the same Lord; and there are varieties of activities, but it is the same God who empowers them all in everyone. To each is given the manifestation of the Spirit for the common good.[157]

After saying that God gives spiritual gifts, Paul begins listing some of them. Found in that list, is one that is not discussed much these days. He writes, "The ability to distinguish between spirits."[158]

I contend that this gift is as needed today as it was in the time of the apostles. We know that our trouble comes at us from a perplexing combination of the world, the flesh, and the devil. Added to that is

---

156 Ephesians 6:18.
157 1 Corinthians 12:4 – 7.
158 1 Corinthians 12:10.

our own personal complexity; we are body, soul, and spirit—with physical, mental, emotional, and spiritual factors all interacting with each other. At times we can be confused, unable to accurately define the source of our problem. To remain alone in situations like that is unnecessary. How helpful it is to have others who are gifted in discernment, with whom we can share our burdens! Their discernment will be used of the Lord to bring the necessary clarity.

I offer one other comment in this regard. Some Christians have a heightened sensitivity to the unseen realm. Often this awareness is linked to past experiences—usually experiences that were dangerous and from which the Lord graciously delivered them. These fellow believers would probably tell you that they wished they had not gone through those trials, but now that they have, they can be a help to others. These people should not be brushed aside when they suggest that there is a demonic element in a situation. It is very possible that they are sensing something real that you and others are missing.

There is more opportunity within the body of Christ for you to receive truth.

The great tactic of our enemy is deception. His nature is to lie, and he is even called "the deceiver of the whole world." When he approached Eve, he attempted to lead her astray. His lies were subtle and carefully chosen. [159] You can count on it: any attack of the evil one will involve deception.

The answer to deception is truth. We each bear responsibility to immerse ourselves in the Word of God so we consistently feed on truth. We also each bear responsibility in times of conflict to wield the sword of the Spirit—the Bible. Nevertheless, when we face trials together, we have the help of our brothers and sisters who can speak truth into our lives. They have a different perspective on our trial than we do. They have the Spirit indwelling them, and he will often prompt them to share certain Scripture passages with us. With more

---

[159]   John 8:44; Revelation 12:9; Genesis 3:1 – 7.

eyes on you and your trial, and with more ears listening to you as you process your difficulty, and more mouths willing to speak truth into you, the trial will be borne more easily until the triumph comes.

Satan will try to keep you alone in your thoughts. A few times I have watched lions hunting herds of antelope. It is the animal that gets separated from the herd that gets devoured. You need to share your thoughts with someone and receive their perspective and the truth that God lays on their heart. We usually hesitate to initiate this kind of vulnerability. We find all sorts of excuses to keep our thoughts to ourselves. But Satan thrives in darkness, and his deception is in your thoughts. Secrecy during struggle is Satan's delight. Find trustworthy ones in the body, and allow them to help you in the battle.

One reason we hesitate is that often there is some sort of failure on our part that is mixed into the attack. We don't know how another person is going to respond if they know our sin. But there is a passage in Proverbs that can help us.

> Whoever conceals his transgressions will not prosper, but he who confesses and forsakes them will obtain mercy.[160]

There is spiritual authority in a church's leadership.

One of the reasons I wanted to share *A Pastor's Story* (chapter 14) with you is that the elders of the church were involved in that situation. Although I do not want to make too much of this point, it would be negligent of me not to remind you that in a functioning local church, there is a spiritual authority that rests in its leadership. Something special happens when elders unite to pray against a work of the devil.

If they do not know about your problem, they will not be praying about it. It could be that similar attacks may be occurring

---

160   Proverbs 28:13.

with others in the congregation. It may be that the leaders need to make decisions and pointedly address certain issues. But none of this will be known or acted upon if you remain silent about your struggle. Elders are charged with the spiritual oversight of your local church, and as such they want to hear and to help you. Allow them to enter into your trial.

In summary, refusing to involve others in your trial is to rob yourself of their help. They will pray with and for you, they will provide needed discernment, they will be channels of God's truth to you, and the spiritual leaders of the church will apply their authority against your enemy. You certainly do not want to forfeit all these benefits. Also, not involving others in your spiritual battle robs them of blessing. Others will grow in their faith as they see victory in your life, and later, when they experience a similar trial, or know someone who does, they will face it with confidence and understanding. You do not want to deprive them of that blessing.

Don't fight alone!

20

A BRIEF WORD
ABOUT FAITH

It is the nature of faith to believe God upon his bare word. 'It will not be,' says sense. 'It cannot be,' says reason. 'It both can and will be,' says faith, 'for I have a promise for it!'

John Trapp

Throughout this book, I've referred to the armor of God and that famous passage of Scripture in Ephesians 6. There is one piece of the armor, however, that I haven't explained. Before drawing attention to it, let's look at that passage in its entirety.

> Finally, be strong in the Lord and in the strength of his might. Put on the whole armor of God, that you may be able to stand against the schemes of the devil. For we do not wrestle against flesh and blood, but against the rulers, against the authorities, against the cosmic powers over this present darkness,

against the spiritual forces of evil in the heavenly places. Therefore take up the whole armor of God, that you may be able to withstand in the evil day, and having done all, to stand firm. Stand therefore, having fastened on the belt of truth, and having put on the breastplate of righteousness, and, as shoes for your feet, having put on the readiness given by the gospel of peace. In all circumstances take up the shield of faith, with which you can extinguish all the flaming darts of the evil one; and take the helmet of salvation, and the sword of the Spirit, which is the word of God, praying at all times in the Spirit, with all prayer and supplication. To that end keep alert with all perseverance, making supplication for all the saints, and also for me, that words may be given to me in opening my mouth boldly to proclaim the mystery of the gospel, for which I am an ambassador in chains, that I may declare it boldly, as I ought to speak.[161]

The Apostle Paul uses the illustration of a Roman soldier to teach us about our conflict with the devil. Just as the soldier wore his armor, so we have spiritual armor that must be appropriated in our battle. Paul supplies names to the soldier's equipment: the belt, the breastplate, the boots, the shield, the helmet, and the sword. These represent truth, righteousness, gospel-readiness, faith, salvation, and the Word of God. Added to that list is the weapon of prayer, which Paul explained without a corresponding piece of Roman armor. If you carefully review all that has been covered so far in this book, you'll realize that I've touched on all the pieces of armor—all of them except one.

---

[161]   Ephesians 6:10 – 20.

Note the unique place of faith.

When Paul mentions the shield of faith, he introduces it differently than all the other pieces of armor. He says, "*In all circumstances* take up the shield of faith."[162] The shield is used in combination with all the other armor. Faith is added to everything else.

When we open our mouths to verbally resist the devil, we need faith: we are believing God's promise that when we resist the devil he will flee. When we find ourselves believing lies, and turn afresh to the Word of God to let it instruct us as to what is indeed true, we need faith: we must believe what we find there. When we intercede for our children and present the promises of Scripture to Heaven for God's help, we need faith: we must believe the God of those promises.

Faith is added to our reading of Scripture, our quoting it, our praying, our evangelism, our struggle with the flesh and the world, our claiming of forgiveness, and our resisting.

The Apostle John acknowledged the place of faith when he wrote, "This is the victory that has overcome the world—our faith."[163]

Paul tells us that it is our faith "with which you can extinguish all the flaming darts of the evil one."[164] During the first century, armies sometimes soaked their arrows in flammable pitch. They would then light the arrows and shoot them at the oncoming soldiers. The large Roman shields to which Paul was referring were often coated with a thick covering that absorbed the arrowheads and extinguished the flames.

By using this picture, Paul is saying that in the spiritual realm there are many and varied attacks that come our way. A trusted Bible commentator writes, "The devil's darts no doubt include his mischievous accusations which inflame our conscience with what

---

[162] Ephesians 6:16.
[163] 1 John 5:4.
[164] Ephesians 6:16.

(if we are sheltering in Christ) can only be called false guilt. Other darts are unsought thoughts of doubt and disobedience, rebellion, lust, malice or fear."[165] I would add that all of the stories that I've shared with you are examples of Satan's darts. He attacks us in a multitude of ways. Our faith is essential for doing away with the enemy's attack.

There have been occasions, while wrestling with temptation or a persistent demonic encroachment on my life, when I come to the realization that I have been half-heartedly resisting. I've been saying the words, "In Jesus' name I resist you," but not really believing God. In times like that, I spiritually shake myself awake, begin earnestly praying, and really believe God for answers. Guess what? In those times I always see the Lord come to my aid.

In all circumstances…faith.

We don't need to feel full of faith. We don't have to have a sense of God's might or his willingness to help. We just need to lean on him and believe—even if our faith seems small.

A distraught father was pleading with Jesus to help his little boy who was tormented by a demon.

> And Jesus asked his father, "How long has this been happening to him?" And he said, "From childhood. And it has often cast him into fire and into water, to destroy him. But if you can do anything, have compassion on us and help us." And Jesus said to him, "'If you can'! All things are possible for one who believes." Immediately the father of the child cried out and said, "I believe; help my unbelief!"[166]

This is one of my favorite stories from the life of Christ. He did not scorn the man or reproach him. He accepted the man's call for

---

165   John Stott, *The Message of Ephesians* (Inter-Varsity Press, Downers Grove, IL:1979), 281.

166   Mark 9:21 – 24.

help. The father didn't feel full of faith, but what faith he had was put in Jesus. That's all it took. Jesus delivered the boy from Satan and gave the boy back to his father.

And so it is with us! With what faith we have, even if we are trembling at the knees or faltering in our understanding, we keep pleading with Jesus and trusting him. He will never let us down. He will always remain faithful to his promises. He will deliver us.

> Because he holds fast to me in love, I will deliver him; I will protect him, because he knows my name. When he calls to me, I will answer him; I will be with him in trouble; I will rescue him and honor him.[167]

---

[167] Psalm 91:14 – 15.

21

THE "EVIL DAY"

*He may look on death with joy, who can look on
forgiveness with faith.*

Thomas Watson

Mixed into that well-known passage about the armor of God is
an intriguing phrase that is often overlooked.

> Therefore take up the whole armor of God, that you
> may be able to withstand *in the evil day*, and having
> done all, to stand firm.[168]

What exactly is *the evil day?* Commentators and theologians
have wrestled with that question and have suggested a variety of
interpretations. This is how I understand it: whenever there is evil,
it's an evil day.

There is, therefore, a sense in which every day is evil. We can
be tempted any day, and when we are faced with a temptation,

---

[168] Ephesians 6:13.

we are faced with evil. That is our evil day, and we stand firm by appropriating all the provision that God has made for us.

There are other times, however, when there is a special presentation of evil, some extraordinary kind of temptation or an outright attack of the evil one. Many of the stories I've shared with you illustrate this kind of situation. Out-of-the-ordinary temptation or attack sometimes comes our way. When that is the case, we find ourselves in an evil day.

The evil day could also be a time of unusual trial that involves suffering—often prolonged suffering. The trial itself isn't necessarily evil, but Satan piggybacks on it and tries to turn it towards his evil purposes. James speaks of the interplay between a trial, which is meant to mature us into spiritual completeness, and a temptation, which is intended to lure us away from the will of God.

> Count it all joy, my brothers, when you meet *trials* of various kinds, for you know that the testing of your faith produces steadfastness. And let steadfastness have its full effect, that you may be perfect and complete, lacking in nothing…. Blessed is the man who remains steadfast under *trial*, for when he has stood the test he will receive the crown of life, which God has promised to those who love him. Let no one say when he is *tempted*, "I am being *tempted* by God," for God cannot be *tempted* with evil, and he himself *tempts* no one.[169]

In the quotation above I've put the words *trial* and *tempted* in italics in order to draw your attention to something that occurs in the original language of the New Testament. When James was writing this letter, he used the same Greek word for *trial* as he did for *temptation*. God may allow a trial into our lives for the purpose of

---

[169] James 1:2 – 4, 12 – 13.

making us better, but Satan enters the scene and tries to turn the trial into a temptation. When that is occurring, that too is our evil day.

Normal temptations make any day an evil day. Unusual temptations or attacks of the evil one constitute an evil day. Trials involving suffering can often devolve into an evil day. In all cases, we find our strength in the Lord and stand firm.

There is, however, one other day that I also think is worthy of being called the evil day. It is a day that we will all experience. William Gurnall, an English pastor who lived in the 1600s, helped me think about this issue. He pointed this out to me in his insightful and spiritually powerful book, *The Christian in Complete Armour*. My experience as a pastor confirms my belief that he is correct. What is the evil day? It is the day we face death.

The day of your death is the evil day, and it is coming.

In the well-loved 23rd psalm, often quoted at funerals, we find the words, "Even though I walk through the valley of the shadow of death, I will fear no evil, for you are with me; your rod and your staff, they comfort me."[170] The need for protection from evil is heightened when in the shadow of death. And that shadow will fall over each one of us.

Let Gurnall expand your thinking concerning the certainty and necessity of death.

> God owes a debt both to the first Adam and to the second [i.e., to Christ]. To the first He owes the wages of his sin; to the second, the reward of His sufferings. The place for full payment of both is the other world. So unless death comes to convey man there, the wicked—who are the posterity of the first Adam—will miss the full pay for their sins. The godly also—who are the seed of Christ—cannot

---

[170]   Psalm 23:4.

receive the whole purchase of His blood until they leave this frame of dust. Before the world began, God promised the Son that His shed blood would purchase eternal life for all who trust in Him. This is the reason why God has made the day of death so sure. In it He discharges both bonds.[171]

So in one sense, the day of our death is a good day. It is a step forward in the plan of God to bring us to himself and overcome every consequence of sin. Perhaps this is part of the reason why the psalmist could say, "Precious in the sight of the Lord is the death of his saints."[172]

But in another sense, it is an evil day. The only reason death must take place is that evil entered the human race. We sinned. As a consequence of our sin, our very bodies are corrupted and the justice of God demands that death must reach each one of us. "Therefore, just as sin came into the world through one man, and death through sin, and so death spread to all men because all sinned."[173] None of us will experience life eternally within this mortal body.[174] At the resurrection we will have a new, changed body in which the fullness of Christ's redemption will be experienced forever.[175] But before that transformation, we must pass through that day that has been necessitated by evil: the day of our death.

That day can be called evil for another reason—it is the final testing ground of the Christian. As such, the enemy of our soul often attacks us severely and mercilessly as we approach our death. Some people are snatched unexpectedly and suddenly out of this world and

---

171 William Gurnall, *The Christian in Complete Armour, Vol. 1* (Carlisle: Banner of Truth, 1986), 1:264.
172 Psalm 116:15.
173 Romans 5:12.
174 See Romans 8:10 – 11.
175 See 1 Corinthians 15:49 – 58.

into the next. But for many others advancing age, declining health, or incurable disease announces to them that the day of their death is approaching. In these cases God has arranged for them to know that they are dying. This is when Satan has his last chance.

If persons in this situation have trusted in Jesus Christ for their salvation, they cannot be turned away from Christ on their deathbed. But it appears that Satan tries to accomplish this nonetheless. At the very least he wants to ruin the Christian's testimony. The devil has the same nature (a liar and a murderer[176]) and the same intent (to steal, kill, and destroy[177]) when we are on our deathbed as he does throughout our lives.

One of his merciless strategies is to remind the dying Christian of his or her sins. Gurnall explains,

> The day of affliction brings unwelcome reminders
> of what sinful evils have passed in our lives. Old sins,
> which were buried many years ago in the grave of
> forgetfulness, come back to haunt us. Their ghosts
> walk in our consciences. And as the darkness of
> night heightens our fear of the unseen, so the day
> when death approaches adds to the terror of our
> sins, then remembered.[178]

It may also be that dying believers become distressed by their own fear of death, and their own daily sin, which their affliction reveals to them. Satan then piles on the insinuations that the suffering person really isn't a Christian after all. Doubts increase, and as Gurnall said in the quote above, the night hours of darkness can be the most troublesome.

---

[176] John 8:44.
[177] John 10:10.
[178] William Gurnall, *The Christian in Complete Armour, Vol. 1*, (Carlisle: Banner of Truth, 1986), 261.

We each need to prepare ourselves for this day.

Why do I make a point of all this? Because we need to make ourselves ready for this evil day. In my experience as a pastor, I have had the privilege to be at the bedside of numerous dying people. In many cases the experience was as much or more of a blessing to me than it was to the person I was visiting. Their faith and the evident grace of God that was bearing them along were notable and marvelous to behold. In other cases there was a real struggle with anxiety, fear, doubt, and an uneasy conscience. But even in these latter cases, as the people submitted to God and reaffirmed their belief, their fear was changed to confidence, their uncertainty changed to faith.

In all cases, however, whether it had happened early or late in their terminal condition, those who overcame the troubling accusations of the evil one did so by focusing on the cross. Satan's accusations about our past and present sins fall powerless before the truths of Calvary.

Peter told us that "he [i.e., Jesus] himself bore our sins in his body on the tree...By his wounds you have been healed."[179] Jesus substituted himself for us. The justice of heaven demanded that lawbreakers pay a penalty. Jesus stood in for the lawbreakers—that's us—and paid our penalty. "All we like sheep have gone astray; we have turned—every one—to his own way; and the Lord has laid on him the iniquity of us all."[180] Heaven accepted this payment, and so we are forgiven.

Thus, we find forgiveness with God, not because of what we have done to earn it, but because Jesus Christ earned it for us. It becomes ours when we put our faith in him. "For by grace you have been saved through faith. And this is not your own doing; it is the gift of God, not a result of works, so that no one may boast."[181]

---

[179] 1 Peter 2:24.

[180] Isaiah 53:6.

[181] Ephesians 2:8 – 9.

If God plans for me to know I am on my deathbed, I plan on fighting the accusations of the devil with the truths of the cross. I will remind him, and myself, of the death of Christ on my behalf. Yes, I am a sinner—past and present—but Jesus Christ bore those sins in his body on the tree! I am forgiven and thus have nothing to fear in death. I'll quote verses that contain these truths at Satan and then say, *"Be gone, Satan! For the Word of God says, 'There is therefore now no condemnation for those who are in Christ Jesus!'"*[182]

I hope that you have a similar confidence about your own death. All the advice contained in this book will not profit you unless you have entered into a personal relationship with Christ—unless you can say with faith, "Jesus bore *my* sins in his body on the tree!"

We need to help each other through it.

Another reason for explaining the evil day to you is that you would be alert to help others as they approach their own death. Dying Christians need other Christians around them. The Scripture says, "Help the weak."[183] Certainly that admonition applies to us when a Christian friend or family member is dying. We need to be with them, to gently remind them of the truths of Christ's payment for sins, and to resist the devil on their behalf.

I remember one occasion when an elderly gentleman was only hours away from death. He had been bedridden for several weeks, and now the end was drawing near. He could no longer speak with us. I stood at his bedside looking down on him and his wife mentioned that he seemed anxious and unsettled. I had noticed it also. Different than the confidence of previous days, he was displaying agitation. I've learned what to do in situations like this, and I want to tell you so that you can do it too. You don't have to be a pastor to do this: anyone in Christ can do so.

---

182   Romans 8:1.
183   1 Thessalonians 5:14.

You bend over with your mouth close to the dying one's ear and pray so that he or she can hear you. Exalt Christ in your prayer. Lift him up. Worship him as the King of kings and Lord of lords. Ask him to help the one who is lying there. Then, momentarily, address the devil. Tell Satan that he has no right to be in that room, troubling the dying one. In the name of Jesus Christ, tell him to leave, and quote Scripture at him. Then turn your attention back to the Lord. Continue to pray, being sensitive to the Spirit's leading.

If you pray in this way, at a time like that, I believe you will see what I have seen. You will see the person begin to calm down, the agitation recede, and peace settle in the room.

I don't know exactly what it will be like when it is my turn to die. But if I'm lying immobile in such a weak state, I will earnestly want to have my brothers and sisters around me—resisting the devil for me, rehearsing the truths of the cross to me, and worshiping the Lord with me.

Together, we can withstand in the evil day, and having done all, to stand firm.

22

THE GOOD ANGELS

Martin Luther explains that angels have a two-fold work; to sing the praises of God on high, and to watch over his saints here below.

John Flavel

So far I have concentrated my attention on the evil aspects of the unseen realm. Lest I give the wrong impression, I want to briefly remind us that evil beings are not the only ones who operate in that realm. There are good beings too. The Scripture calls them angels.

Just like everything else that exists, angels are created beings. They have not existed from eternity past. Only our Triune God is from everlasting and to everlasting.[184]

The mystery concerning the unseen realm applies to the good angels also. God does not satisfy all our curiosity. But Scripture does give us important information, and that information increases our confidence in the wisdom, might, protection, and steadfast love of God.

---

[184]   Psalm 90:2.

Some Bible commentators estimate that there are over 300 references to angels in the Bible. From the Old Testament through the New, we see God using angels, and we see them glorifying God through their obedience and worship. It is not my aim here to summarize all that the Bible teaches concerning angels. But I do want to answer three questions in order to increase our confidence and guard us from one particularly dangerous error.

What is the relationship between the good angels and the demons?

Pastors, theologians, and Bible students from all eras of history and all nations have pointed to three passages of Scripture as the foundation for our understanding of how Satan and the demons came to be. These passages are found in Ezekiel, Isaiah, and Revelation.

The prophet Ezekiel once spoke against the king of Tyre, but his words had a double meaning. Not only was he addressing the fall of Tyre's king but he was also describing the fall of one of the angels.

> Son of man, raise a lamentation over the king of Tyre, and say to him, "Thus says the Lord God: 'You were the signet of perfection, full of wisdom and perfect in beauty. You were in Eden, the garden of God; every precious stone was your covering, sardius, topaz, and diamond, beryl, onyx, and jasper, sapphire, emerald, and carbuncle; and crafted in gold were your settings and your engravings. On the day that you were created they were prepared. You were an anointed guardian cherub. I placed you; you were on the holy mountain of God; in the midst of the stones of fire you walked. You were blameless in your ways from the day you were created, till unrighteousness was found in you. In the abundance of your trade you were filled with violence in your midst, and you sinned; so I cast you

as a profane thing from the mountain of God, and I destroyed you, O guardian cherub, from the midst of the stones of fire. Your heart was proud because of your beauty; you corrupted your wisdom for the sake of your splendor. I cast you to the ground; I exposed you before kings, to feast their eyes on you.'"[185]

In Ezekiel's words, we see God addressing a created being—a cherub. This angel was created good. He was an exceptional creature, endowed by God with noteworthy beauty and power—possibly even exceeding that of all other angels. But he became proud and attempted something that was motivated by his desire for his own splendor. God did not allow this attempt to succeed. The mighty angel was "cast to the ground."

When the prophet Isaiah spoke against the king of Babylon, his words also had a double meaning. Not only was he addressing the fall of Babylon's human king; but he was also describing the fall of one of the angels. We understand it as being the same angel that is described in Ezekiel. In Isaiah's description we learn more about the inner motivation of this erring angel.

How you are fallen from heaven, O Day Star, son of Dawn! How you are cut down to the ground, you who laid the nations low! You said in your heart, "I will ascend to heaven; above the stars of God I will set my throne on high; I will sit on the mount of assembly in the far reaches of the north; I will ascend above the heights of the clouds; I will make myself like the Most High." But you are brought down to Sheol, to the far reaches of the pit.[186]

---

[185]   Ezekiel 28:12 – 17.
[186]   Isaiah 14:12 – 15.

In these words of Isaiah, we see that this angel began to covet God's place. He wanted to be seated on God's throne. This one wanted to make himself "like the Most High." There was rebellion in this angel's heart, but God did not allow that rebellion to remain in heaven. The angel was "brought down."

We understand these two portions of God's Word to be teaching us that Satan was created as a good angel but rebelled against God. We do not have many details of this rebellion. We are left with unanswered questions. But that's okay; if the Lord doesn't give us answers to some of our questions, it is because we don't need those answers. Nevertheless, this we do know about Satan—he is a mighty angel who was initially good but is now in rebellion against God.

The book of Revelation adds some more details to the story. The mighty cherub of Ezekiel, the Day Star of Isaiah, did not rebel alone.

> And another sign appeared in heaven: behold, a great red dragon, with seven heads and ten horns, and on his heads seven diadems. His tail swept down a third of the stars of heaven and cast them to the earth.[187]

The "stars" in this passage represent other angels. When the dragon, who is Satan, was cast out of heaven, he took a third of the angels with him. They are the ones that Scripture refers to as demons, evil spirits, or unclean spirits.

We see no evidence in Scripture that there is still a possibility of more good angels rebelling, or of the fallen angels repenting. Since the time when Satan and a third of the angels were cast out of heaven, there have been two fixed groups of angelic beings: those who remain faithful, and those who have rebelled. The unseen realm is the normal sphere of operations for all of them: both good angels and demons. Both are in the spiritual realm. Both are active. The result, of course, is war.

---

[187] Revelation 12:3 – 4.

Now war arose in heaven, Michael and his angels fighting against the dragon. And the dragon and his angels fought back, but he was defeated, and there was no longer any place for them in heaven. And the great dragon was thrown down, that ancient serpent, who is called the devil and Satan, the deceiver of the whole world—he was thrown down to the earth, and his angels were thrown down with him. And I heard a loud voice in heaven, saying, "Now the salvation and the power and the kingdom of our God and the authority of his Christ have come, for the accuser of our brothers has been thrown down, who accuses them day and night before our God. And they have conquered him by the blood of the Lamb and by the word of their testimony, for they loved not their lives even unto death. Therefore, rejoice, O heavens and you who dwell in them! But woe to you, O earth and sea, for the devil has come down to you in great wrath, because he knows that his time is short!"[188]

That war has come to earth, and it is the one in which we are engaged. It is the one that the pages of this book are explaining. And, hallelujah, it is the one that will end with total victory for the Lord Jesus!

What do the good angels do for us in our struggle against the evil one?

We can say with conviction that angels help God's people. In his famous comparison of Christ and the angels, the author of the book of Hebrews says, "Are they not all ministering spirits sent out to serve for the sake of those who are to inherit salvation?"[189] In that Scripture

---

[188]   Revelation 12:7 – 12.
[189]   Hebrews 1:14.

passage the author does not give us details on *how* the angels help us, but his point is very clear: God sends angels to help his people.

The kind of help that Scripture specifically mentions is protection. Note that in both of the following verses from the Psalms, we are told that angels are used by God to protect us.

> The angel of the Lord encamps around those who fear him, and delivers them.[190]

> For he will command his angels concerning you to guard you in all your ways.[191]

We do not know how much of the time God uses his angels to protect us and how much of the time he protects us without using angels. I suspect that he does both. But in the above psalms we are taught that God does indeed, at least some of the time, use angels for our deliverance.

If we know this is true, we can participate in it through prayer. A large part of growing in prayer is learning to align our requests with what we know of God. Once I realized that God sends angels to guard his people, I began incorporating that concept into my prayers, especially when I was afraid of danger. I would pray, "Lord, give your angels a command concerning us! Protect us, Lord!" I have found that taking the language of those psalms and using them in prayer gives strength and encouragement. I also have seen great protection from danger.[192] Behind the scenes, in the realm that I cannot see, I am sure that there have been angels protecting me, my family, and the churches in which I have served.

I have been trying to alert you to the reality and power of the unseen realm. By necessity, I have been drawing some attention to Satan and the demons. But the unseen realm doesn't belong to

---

190 Psalm 34:7.

191 Psalm 91:11.

192 I explained in chapter 14 how I use Psalm 91:11 in prayer for our children.

Satan. It is the Lord's, and it contains a host of good angels that are tasked to help you and me!

It is worth noting that the angels greatly outnumber the demons. In Revelation 12 we read, "His tail swept down a third of the stars of heaven and cast them to the earth."[193] I'm not sure if the phrase "a third" was meant in a mathematically-precise way. What it does make clear, however, is that there are overwhelmingly more good angels than bad! Think of it! As intimidating as it is to imagine there being unseen demons near you, it is even more exciting to realize that there are at least twice as many unseen good angels nearby.

This truth is illustrated in one of the events in the prophet Elisha's life. The king of Syria had sent his army to find and kill Elisha.

> When the servant of the man of God rose early in the morning and went out, behold, an army with horses and chariots was all around the city. And the servant said, "Alas, my master! What shall we do?" He said, "Do not be afraid, for those who are with us are more than those who are with them." Then Elisha prayed and said, "O Lord, please open his eyes that he may see." So the Lord opened the eyes of the young man, and he saw, and behold, the mountain was full of horses and chariots of fire all around Elisha.[194]

Indeed, it isn't so much the appearance of the angels or their power that is emphasized in that story, but their *number.* "Those that are with us are more than those who are with them."

So, as you think through the issues I've raised, please remember that the "good guys" outnumber the "bad guys!" Don't let your new awareness and knowledge about our spiritual conflict create a

---

193   Revelation 12:3 – 4.
194   2 Kings 6:15 – 17.

mindset of being fearfully surrounded with unseen foes. Yes, those foes are a reality, but so is our Lord and his host of angels!

Do I try to contact angels?

There is an alarming teaching in some forms of Christianity that encourages people to pray to angels. This is a false teaching that carries grave danger for those who practice it.

Scripture does not teach us to seek communication with angels. Although there are a few instances in the psalms in which the psalmist is exhorting the angels to worship the Lord, these verses cannot be used to support the idea of *praying* to angels. [195] These examples in the psalms are not requests, nor the initiation of a two-way communication. They were brief expressions of the worthiness of God.

There are no permissions given us in Scripture for seeking to communicate with unseen angelic beings. None. To the contrary, prohibitions such as Deuteronomy 18:10 – 12[196] make it clear that any attempt to communicate with beings in the unseen realm is forbidden. We are not taught to initiate contact with the good angels. Our only reach into the unseen realm is to talk to God in the name of Jesus Christ.

If there are good angels, and they are sent to help us, why should it be forbidden to try to communicate with them? There are many reasons, but one of great importance involves the combination of our gullibility and Satan's ability. The Apostle Paul warned the Christians in Corinth about false apostles. He pointed out the fact that evil people can appear to be good people.

> And no wonder, for even Satan disguises himself as
> an angel of light.[197]

---

[195] Psalm 29:1; 103:20; 148:2.
[196] Deuteronomy 18:10 – 12.
[197] 2 Corinthians 11:14.

Satan can make himself look like a good angel. His ability to deceive is formidable. People who are mistakenly encouraged to seek to speak to angels can have emotional experiences with what they initially perceive to be a good angel, and later they realize that they have become entangled in the powerful deception of a demon.

And besides, why would we need to pray to an angel? The God of heaven and earth delivered his only Son to the agony of the cross in order to reconcile us to himself. He then invites us to speak directly to himself in the name of that crucified and risen Son. We have no need to pray to any entity, human or angel, except God himself!

And when we pray, God answers! Sometimes his answers involve sending angels to our aid. We don't normally see them, but it is happening nonetheless. Oh, the wisdom, might, protection, and steadfast love of God! Because of God and his angels, we engage in our spiritual conflict with the confidence that we are safe and on the winning side!

23

CHRIST VICTORIOUS

*Fear not, I am the first and the last, and the living
one. I died, and behold I am alive forevermore,
and I have the keys of Death and Hades.*
                                    Jesus Christ the Lord

I began this book by pointing out that we do not read very far into
Genesis before being introduced to Satan. I want to end this book
by showing you that from that very point onward, the Scriptures
show with increasing momentum and clarity that Christ *is* victorious
over Satan. It is true that we have a formidable foe, but it is supremely
true that Jesus Christ has defeated that foe.

Soon after Satan's success in the Garden of Eden, the Lord
confronts him. What God says in that confrontation is very
important.

> The Lord God said to the serpent, "Because you
> have done this, cursed are you...I will put enmity
> between you and the woman, and between your

offspring and her offspring; he shall bruise your head, and you shall bruise his heel."[198]

Notice the words about bruising the head and the heel. The Hebrew word translated as "bruise" can also be translated "crush." This is a foretelling of the future. A special descendant of Eve would one day come. Satan would injure him (bruise his heel), but the special one would destroy Satan (crush his head).

In the book of Job, we see another foretelling of the future. This triumphant prophecy tells us that Leviathan, as Satan is referred to in Job, would be silenced.[199] Although our finite minds cannot understand how it is that God allows and uses evil, we can rest in the fact that He has determined to bring it to an end. Leviathan will be silenced![200]

In those prophecies we are not told any details concerning *how* our enemy would be silenced, only *that* he would be. But later in the Old Testament, we see a prophetic vision that hints at how the special descendant of Eve would do it. The prophet Zechariah says,

> Then he showed me Joshua the high priest standing before the angel of the Lord, and Satan standing at his right hand to accuse him. And the Lord said to Satan, "The Lord rebuke you, O Satan! The Lord who has chosen Jerusalem rebuke you! Is not this a brand plucked from the fire?" Now Joshua was standing before the angel, clothed with filthy garments. And the angel said to those who were standing before him, "Remove the filthy garments from him." And to him he said, "Behold, I have taken your iniquity away from you, and I will clothe you with pure vestments." And I said, "Let them

---

[198]   Genesis 3:14 – 15.

[199]   I have explained this in more detail in chapter 10.

[200]   This teaching can be seen in Job 41, and is reinforced by Isaiah 27:1.

put a clean turban on his head." So they put a clean
turban on his head and clothed him with garments.
And the angel of the Lord was standing by.[201]

Zechariah's prophecy shows us that the accuser will lose his
leverage over the sinner because the Lord would take away the
sinner's filth and put purity in its place. All of this would happen
in a legal way. Before the Judge of Heaven, some sort of transaction
would take place. This transaction would cleanse the sinner, and
thus the accusations of the accuser would cease.

We have to wait for the New Testament to understand more
completely these prophetic glimpses of Satan's downfall and our Lord's
victory. Nevertheless, we close the Old Testament with a clear picture
that God would defeat Satan, fully and finally, through a special
descendant of Eve and do so through a transaction concerning our sin.

When we turn to the New Testament, we immediately find that
all four Gospels make it abundantly clear that Jesus of Nazareth,
born of the Virgin Mary, legal son of Joseph, descendant of David,
is the long hoped-for Messiah. Jesus is the Christ, the Anointed
One, the Son of God and Son of Man, the focal point of all the Old
Testament prophecies about God's victory over Satan.

The apostle John said that "the reason the Son of God appeared
was to destroy the works of the devil."[202] The destruction of Satan's
work began immediately upon Jesus' coming.

Jesus was victorious over the devil in his initial temptation in
the wilderness.[203] Weakened by a long fast, Jesus nevertheless fended
off the repeated temptations with which Satan personally presented
him. Only one sin and Jesus would have been disqualified to be the
Savior and King. But he did not sin, and the devil left in defeat.

Jesus was victorious over the devil by casting demons out of
many people and healing them of diseases that were due to demonic

---

201   Zechariah 3:1 – 5.
202   1 John 3:8.
203   Matthew 4:1 – 11; Luke 4:1 – 13.

influence. There are several occurrences in the Gospels in which a general statement is made about this phenomenon.[204] I give you one here:

> So his fame spread throughout all Syria, and they brought him all the sick, those afflicted with various diseases and pains, those oppressed by demons, epileptics, and paralytics, and he healed them.[205]

But the Gospel authors did more than record these encounters in a general way. They also showed us the details of one encounter after another, and in those details, we see the victorious Christ dismantling the work of the devil.

Early in Christ's ministry, the demons screamed out his identity. They knew who he was and knew that they were at his mercy.

> And in the synagogue there was a man who had the spirit of an unclean demon, and he cried out with a loud voice, "Ha! What have you to do with us, Jesus of Nazareth? Have you come to destroy us? I know who you are—the Holy One of God." But Jesus rebuked him, saying, "Be silent and come out of him!" And when the demon had thrown him down in their midst, he came out of him, having done him no harm. And they were all amazed and said to one another, "What is this word? For with authority and power he commands the unclean spirits, and they come out!"[206]

---

204 Some references made in a general way are: Matthew 4:24; 8:16; Mark 1:32 – 34; 3:11; Luke 6:18.

205 Matthew 4:24.

206 Luke 4:33 – 36. This account is also found in Mark 1:23 – 28.

The Gerasene demoniacs, filled with multiple demons, could not be tamed by men or chains, yet these tormented men were freed by Christ.[207] A mute man spoke after Jesus confronted the demon inside him.[208] And then later, "a demon-oppressed man who was blind and mute was brought to him, and he healed him, so that the man spoke and saw."[209] No affliction that the devil brought on a human being could not be undone by Jesus!

The little Jewish boy with demonically-caused seizures and the little Gentile girl oppressed by a demon were both healed by an authoritative word of Christ.[210] A crippled woman, disfigured for almost two decades by the affliction of Satan, stood up straight and healthy because Jesus laid his hands on her and commanded that she be healed.[211] And Mary Magdalene, one of Jesus' most faithful followers, had been possessed by demons when she first met him.[212] She was ever after known as "the one from whom seven demons had gone out."[213] Jesus was not only setting people free, but he was also making them his followers!

So significant was this ministry of Jesus that when the imprisoned John the Baptist sent for confirmation concerning Jesus' identity, Jesus pointed to the confrontations with the devil as part of the proof that he was the one whom Scripture had foretold.

> And when the men had come to him, they said, "John the Baptist has sent us to you, saying, 'Are you the one who is to come, or shall we look for

---

207   Matthew 8:28 – 34; Mark 5:1 – 20; Luke 8:26 – 33.

208   Matthew 9:32 – 33; Luke 11:14.

209   Matthew 12:22.

210   The Syrophoenician woman's daughter: Matthew 15:21 – 28; Mark 7:24 – 30. The Jewish man's son: Matthew 17:15 – 18; Mark 9:14 – 29; Luke 9:37 – 42.

211   Luke 13:10 – 17.

212   Mark 16:9; Luke 8:2.

213   Luke 8:2.

another?'" In that hour he healed many people of diseases and plagues and evil spirits, and on many who were blind he bestowed sight. And he answered them, "Go and tell John what you have seen and heard."[214]

The work of Satan was being destroyed, and Jesus was the one who was doing it!

Jesus then expanded his victory. He commissioned his disciples to confront the demons and gave them the authority to do so. First, he did this with the Twelve,[215] and then with seventy-two of his followers.[216] Their awe-filled report about their success against the devil gave Jesus an opportunity to give insight about his victory.

The seventy-two returned with joy, saying, "Lord, even the demons are subject to us in your name!" And he said to them, "I saw Satan fall like lightning from heaven."[217]

I believe that Jesus was referencing the events of Revelation 12, when Satan was cast out of heaven. He fell like lightening—and Jesus was there to see it. The verb tense in the Greek word translated "fall" refers to an action that was in the past but has ongoing ramifications. In this account Jesus had just authorized his followers to go and confront the demons in his name. They did so, and Satan's hold on the people of that area was being loosened. The devil's work was being destroyed. The ramifications of his lightning-quick fall from heaven were growing ever larger.

Jesus, through his disciples, was now continuing his victory over the devil!

---

214 Luke 7:20 – 23.
215 Matthew 10:8; Mark 3:15; 6:7; Luke 9:1.
216 Luke 10:17,19.
217 Luke 10:17 – 18.

Satan then attempted to divert Jesus.

> From that time Jesus began to show his disciples
> that he must go to Jerusalem and suffer many
> things from the elders and chief priests and scribes,
> and be killed, and on the third day be raised. And
> Peter took him aside and began to rebuke him,
> saying, "Far be it from you, Lord! This shall never
> happen to you." But he turned and said to Peter,
> "Get behind me, Satan! You are a hindrance to me.
> For you are not setting your mind on the things of
> God, but on the things of man."[218]

Knowing that the foundation of our salvation and Satan's defeat
is in Christ's death, we understand that Jesus was not being overly
stern with Peter. Satan was the originator of Peter's idea. It was a
satanic suggestion that Jesus could somehow avoid dying and rising
again. Although Peter had just recently expressed great faith and was
unquestionably one of Jesus' closest disciples, he was momentarily
used by Satan. Jesus recognized this devilish attack and responded
accordingly.

Jesus was victorious once more!

And he would be victorious again, this time in all of Satan's
attempts to attack him during his experience of the cross. Jesus had
earlier said that one of his disciples would be used by the devil.[219]
It was the devil who put the idea of betrayal into Judas Iscariot's
heart, and Jesus knew that it was happening.[220] When he and the
disciples were preparing to leave the upper room for the Garden of
Gethsemane, Jesus knew that another encounter with Satan was
imminent.[221]

---

[218] Matthew 16:21 – 23. This account is also found in Mark 8:31 – 33.
[219] John 6:70.
[220] Luke 22:3 – 6; John 13:2,27.
[221] John 14:30.

Having failed to divert Jesus *from* the cross, Satan would now attempt to use the circumstances *of* the cross to tempt him. But Jesus was ready for him and did not succumb.

Although it is not explicitly stated in Scripture, I have reason to believe that the devil was tempting Jesus all through the events of that night and the next day. In Gethsemane Christ faced the reality of his upcoming suffering. Luke records, "And being in an agony he prayed more earnestly; and his sweat became like great drops of blood falling down to the ground."[222] I can easily imagine the same one who, in the wilderness, took Jesus up and "showed him all the kingdoms of the world in a moment of time, and said to him, 'If you, then, will worship me, it will all be yours,'"[223] that same one was tempting Jesus during his suffering. The devilish suggestion probably came repeatedly—the kingdoms of the world could belong to Christ in a way that would avoid the suffering of the cross.

And so, throughout the desertion and denial of his disciples, the beatings and merciless torture of the Roman soldiers, the cries of "crucify him!" from the crowd, the mocking taunts at the height of his pain—" He saved others; he cannot save himself. He is the King of Israel; let him come down now from the cross, and we will believe in him."[224]—through it all, the Lord Jesus remained faithful.

> And being found in human form, he humbled
> himself by becoming obedient to the point of death,
> even death on a cross.[225]

When he cried "It is finished!" he sealed his obedience on the cross. He gave up his spirit, breathed his last, and died in obedience—sinless and victorious over every temptation that Satan could hurl his way.

---

[222] Luke 22:44.

[223] Luke 4:5 – 7.

[224] Matthew 27:42.

[225] Philippians 2:8.

Although to the eyes of flesh it appeared that he had just been defeated, he had won. He had fulfilled what the prophet Zechariah had foretold. Before the Judge of Heaven, the accuser could no longer point his finger at a sinner and demand his death. Our advocate, the Christ, had substituted himself for us and received upon himself all the punishment that we rightfully deserved for our sin. On the cross, he exhausted the wrath of God on our account. He satisfied the justice of God. No more penalty is demanded by the holiness of God. It has all been meted out upon the substitute. Then, the righteousness of Christ is placed upon the sinner. Just like the picture in Zechariah, our filthy garments are removed and clean ones replace them.

Satan used to have the power of death over us, the ability to demand our eternal condemnation. But Jesus has disarmed him, taking away his only claim on us.

> Since therefore the children [i.e., human beings] share in flesh and blood, he himself likewise partook of the same things, that through death he might destroy the one who has the power of death, that is, the devil, and deliver all those who through fear of death were subject to lifelong slavery.[226]

There is no longer a heavenly warrant out for our arrest and punishment. That has been erased by the death of Christ.

> And you, who were dead in your trespasses ..., God made alive together with him, having forgiven us all our trespasses, by canceling the record of debt that stood against us with its legal demands. This he set aside, nailing it to the cross. He disarmed the

---

[226] Hebrews 2:14 – 15.

rulers and authorities and put them to open shame,
by triumphing over them in him.[227]

You see, Satan's power against us is linked to our guilt before
God, but Christ took that guilt away by his death on the cross.
Satan, therefore, has lost that leverage he had over us. He has no
right to exercise any influence on us again. If we are in Christ, we
are set free.

> He [i.e., God] has delivered us from the domain
> of darkness and transferred us to the kingdom of
> his beloved Son, in whom we have redemption, the
> forgiveness of sins.[228]

All that Christ accomplished on the cross was validated through
his resurrection. The crucified Christ is vindicated by the empty
tomb. Death could not keep him in its grasp, and his resurrection
and ascension proclaim his victory over evil.

> That he [i.e. God] worked in Christ when he
> raised him from the dead and seated him at his
> right hand in the heavenly places, far above all rule
> and authority and power and dominion, and above
> every name that is named, not only in this age but
> also in the one to come.[229]

Christ is the Victorious One! He disarmed and defeated the
devil through his death on the cross!
The struggle continued, however, because the time for Satan's
complete removal from the scene had not yet come. The early

---

[227] Colossians 2:13 – 15.

[228] Colossians 1:13 – 14.

[229] Ephesians 1:20 – 21.

Christians wrestled and stood firm and resisted, and through them Christ continued to manifest his victory over the evil one.

When the author of the book of Hebrews said that "through death he [i.e. Christ] might destroy the one who has the power of death, that is, the devil," it is important to understand what he meant. The Greek word translated "destroy" is a tricky word to put into English. It has the idea of reducing something to the point where it is ineffective. It has lost its strength, but it is still there. It has not been obliterated but rendered powerless. So it is with the devil—he is still around after his defeat at the cross, but he has lost his power over us. As I said in chapter 5, Satan will attempt to gain footholds in our lives even though he has no right to do so. Therefore, the wrestling continues.

The apostles continued to manifest Christ's victory in that wrestling. "The people also gathered from the towns around Jerusalem, bringing the sick and those afflicted with unclean spirits, and they were all healed."[230] As the gospel spread from Jerusalem to Samaria and the Gentile world, encounters with the demonic showed the ongoing defeat of Satan by Christ.[231] When confronted in the name of Jesus Christ, the evil spirits fled.

The apostles began teaching the early Christians about the struggle with evil—that they must stand firm, resist, and wrestle. Their teaching is found in the New Testament. They wrote about this conflict with optimism and even a hint of joy. They were not retreating with fear but advancing with confidence.

> The God of peace will soon crush Satan under your feet! The grace of our Lord Jesus Christ be with you![232]

---

[230] Acts 5:16.
[231] Acts 8:4 – 8; 19:11 – 20.
[232] Romans 16:20.

And no wonder they were so confident: they understood that the ground of their victory was in the death of Christ, they had seen Christ model spiritual warfare for them, and they had experienced the wrestling and the victory themselves. But there was one more reason why they were so infectiously optimistic—they knew that Christ was coming back to bring to completion his defeat of evil!

They knew that they were living in the "in-between." Satan was defeated but not yet completely out of the picture. But this reality is only for a time. The Lord Jesus will one day come back and absolutely do away with the devil.

The foundation of Christ's victory is the cross. The culmination of his victory is in the final days. Those days are shown to us in the book of Revelation.

> Then I saw an angel coming down from heaven, holding in his hand the key to the bottomless pit and a great chain. And he seized the dragon, that ancient serpent, who is the devil and Satan, and bound him for a thousand years, and threw him into the pit, and shut it and sealed it over him, so that he might not deceive the nations any longer, until the thousand years were ended. After that he must be released for a little while…. And when the thousand years are ended, Satan will be released from his prison and will come out to deceive the nations that are at the four corners of the earth, Gog and Magog, to gather them for battle; their number is like the sand of the sea. And they marched up over the broad plain of the earth and surrounded the camp of the saints and the beloved city, but fire came down from heaven and consumed them, and the devil who had deceived them was thrown into the lake of fire and sulfur where the beast and the

false prophet were, and they will be tormented day
and night forever and ever.[233]

God told the apostles, and is telling us, that there is coming a
day when the devil will be put away from us and punished forever.
Beginning on that day there will be no more wrestling or resisting
because our enemy will be completely out of our experience.
Leviathan will be finally silenced. The decisive defeat of the cross
will be brought to its ultimate consummation. Satan will not only
be rendered powerless but be put away completely. The "in-between"
wrestling will be over. We will be experiencing the new heavens and
the new earth, and evil will no longer be present.

> Then I saw a new heaven and a new earth, for the
> first heaven and the first earth had passed away, and
> the sea was no more. And I saw the holy city, new
> Jerusalem, coming down out of heaven from God,
> prepared as a bride adorned for her husband. And I
> heard a loud voice from the throne saying, "Behold,
> the dwelling place of God is with man. He will
> dwell with them, and they will be his people, and
> God himself will be with them as their God. He
> will wipe away every tear from their eyes, and death
> shall be no more, neither shall there be mourning,
> nor crying, nor pain anymore, for the former things
> have passed away."[234]

And who will do this wondrous thing? Our Lord Jesus Christ!

> And he who was seated on the throne said, "Behold,
> I am making all things new."...And he said to me,

---

[233] Revelation 20:1 – 3, 7 – 10.
[234] Revelation 21:1 – 4.

"It is done! I am the Alpha and the Omega, the beginning and the end."[235]

It is Christ, the Victorious One! The Lamb of God who took away the sins of the world, the King of kings and Lord of lords, it is he who vanquishes evil! And it is he who we will see and adore and worship.

No longer will there be anything accursed, but the throne of God and of the Lamb will be in it, and his servants will worship him. They will see his face, and his name will be on their foreheads. And night will be no more.[236]

That day is coming. Christ Victorious will be in our gaze, and we will love him without being troubled by evil. Our hearts will be filled with admiration and gratitude for all he has done against the evil one on our behalf. He will be there, in our midst, the one who died for us, the one who cast the devil into the pit forevermore.

Hallelujah!

---

[235] Revelation 21:5 – 6.
[236] Revelation 22:3 – 5.

BIBLIOGRAPHY

Anderson, Neil., *The Bondage Breaker.,* Eugene: Harvest House Publishers, 1990.

Berkhof, Louis. *Systematic Theology.,* Grand Rapids: Eerdmans Publishing, 1981.

Black, Rob. *Picture This: Diagrams to Make Scriptural Truths Clear.,* 3rd ed., Published by Author, 2014.

Bubeck, Mark I. *The Adversary.,* Chicago: Moody Press, 1975.

Burchett, Harold. *People Helping People.,* Chicago: Moody Press, 1979.

Burchett, Harold. *Spiritual Life Studies.* 2nd ed., Published by Author, 2000.

Buswell, J. Oliver. *A Systematic Theology of the Christian Religion.,* Singapore: Christian Life Publishers, 1994.

Grudem, Wayne. *Systematic Theology.,* Grand Rapids: Zondervan, 1994.

Gurnall, William. *The Christian in Complete Armour, Vol. 1.,* Carlisle: Banner of Truth, 1986.

185

Cairns, Alan. *Dictionary of Theological Terms.*, Greenville: Ambassador Emerald International, 2002.

Plumer, William S. *Psalms: A Critical and Expository Commentary with Doctrinal and Practical Remarks.*, Carlisle: Banner of Truth, 1975.

Stott, John. *The Message of Ephesians.*, Downers Grove: Inter-Varsity Press, 1979.

SCRIPTURE INDEX